초급 한국어 말하기
Speaking Korean for beginners

발간사

'외국인을 위한 한국어 교재'를 발행하며

한국어는 이제 전 세계 70개 국의 중·고등학교와 대학, 그리고 일반 성인들이 학습하는 세계 10대 언어에 속하는 국제어의 위상을 가지고 있는 언어입니다. 또한 650만 명의 재외 국민 자녀들이 주말학교 등에서 다양한 방법으로 한국어를 배우고 있습니다. 이와 같은 한국어의 문자인 한글은 세계문화유산에 등재된 인류의 위대한 문화유산입니다.

또한 국제 업무의 원활화, 월드컵 영향, 한류, 관광 등 한국에 대한 관심이 높아져 많은 외국인들이 한국어를 학습하고 있으며 또한 한국어 배우기를 원하고 있는 사람들의 수 또한 과거에 비해 월등하게 많아지고 있습니다. 이러한 때에 한국어를 좀 더 쉽고 체계적으로 배울 수 있도록 하는 교재의 필요성은 학습자와 교사 모두에게 절실하다고 할 수 있습니다. 따라서 이 교재는 그러한 학습자와 교사의 요구에 바탕을 두고 개발되었다고 할 수 있습니다.

그동안 한국어 교재는 많은 기관과 개인에 의해 만들어졌습니다. 그러나 그것은 기관의 성격이나 국가별 특성이 드러나 세계의 모든 한국어 학습자들이 자유롭게 사용하는 데에는 어려움이 있는 것도 사실이었습니다. 이번 한국어세계화재단에서 개발한 이 교재들은 세계의 어느 나라에서나 현지에서 자유롭게 구매할 수 있고 다양한 형태의 교재로 재구성하여 사용할 수 있도록 특별히 국고를 들여 제작한 것입니다. 또한 어느 특정한 집단을 고려하지 않고 누구나 한국어 학습을 원하는 사람에게 사용될 수 있도록 범용 교재로 편찬하였습니다.

그간 교재들은 듣기·말하기·읽기·쓰기의 통합 교재들이 많아 그것이 가진 장점에도 불구하고 각각의 언어 기능을 독립적으로 강조하거나 또는 기능들 간에 유기적인 관계를 유지하면서 체계적인 학습이 되도록 하기에 어려움이 있었다고 할 수 있습니다. 이 교재는 한국어를 처음 접하는 학습자들이 쉬우면서도 체계적으로 학습할 수 있도록 하는 데 목적을 두고 편찬되었습니다. 우선 듣기·말하기·읽기·쓰기의 네 가지 영역으로 분리하여 초급 학습자들에게 필요한 주제와 기능을 선정하고 이에 따른 학습 어휘와 문법, 그리고 연습 활동과 과제를 제시하였습니다. 그리고 과정 중심 학습을 통해 한국어를 정확하게 학습할 수 있도록 하는 데에도 노력하였습니다.

이 교재는 단원 앞에 학습할 목표를 제시하고 다양한 그림 자료를 활용해 스키마를 형성할 수 있도록 하였으며, 단원 중간이나 마지막 부분에 관련 문화를 설명하고, 마지막에 자기 평가를 할 수 있도록 하는 등 처음부터 마무리까지 학습자 스스로가 주도적인 역할을 할 수 있는 교재를 편찬하기 위해 노력하였습니다. 교재에 사용된 다양한 삽화와 사진들은 한국어를 학습하고 교수하는 데 자료로 활용될 수 있도록 배려한 것입니다. 따라서 이 교재는 말하기, 듣기, 읽기, 쓰기 등 언어 기능별로 독립적으로 학습하고 교수하는 데에도 용이하며 관련된 주제와 기능을 통합하여 학습하고 교수할 수 있는 장점을 가지고 있습니다. 이 교재는 우선 영어로 번역되어 출판되나 곧 다양한 언어로 번역되어 출간될 예정이며 이후 학습자 워크북과 교사 지침서도 발간될 예정입니다. 따라서 다양한 언어권의 한국어 학습자와 교사들을 위해 널리 활용될 수 있을 것으로 확신합니다.

이 교재를 편찬하기 위한 기획 및 개발은 1999년부터 시작되었습니다. 그동안 고려대 김정숙 교수와 이화여대 이해영 교수의 책임하에 많은 연구진들의 노력으로 개발이 진행되었습니다. 당초 목적은 2001년에 실물 교재로 출판하는 것이었으나 내용을 좀 더 다듬고 보완하여 완성도 높은 교재를 제작하기 위한 노력이 진행되어 오늘에 이르러서야 교재를 발간하게 되었습니다.

그리고 이 교재의 발간이 한국어 교육의 활성화를 위한 기폭제가 되기를 기대합니다. 우리 재단에서는 이 교재의 발간에 만족하지 않고 곧 중급, 고급의 한국어 학습 교재를 지속적으로 개발할 것을 약속드립니다. 이러한 약속을 지키는 데에는 이 교재를 사용하는 모든 분들의 관심과 배려가 필요합니다.

이 교재를 발간하게 되기까지에는 많은 분들의 노고가 있었습니다. 우선 국고보조금의 지원과 함께 꾸준한 관심과 애정으로 인내심을 가지고 이 교재의 발간을 기다려 준 문화관광부와 국립국어원에 감사의 말씀을 드립니다. 또한 교재를 개발하기 위해서 처음부터 기획과 연구에 많은 정성을 쏟은 '한국어세계화추진위원회'의 관계자 및 한국어 교육 현장에서 교재의 발간을 기다려 주신 한국어 교사 및 한국어 학습자에게도 감사의 말씀을 드립니다. 그리고 이 교재를 알차게 펴내 주신 한림출판사에도 무한한 감사를 드리는 바입니다.

아무쪼록 이 교재가 한국어를 배우고 가르치는 모든 분들에게 작은 도움이라도 되기를 바라며, 한국어가 전 세계에 보급되는 밑거름이 되기를 간절히 기원합니다.

2006년 3월 10일
재단법인 한국어세계화재단 이사장 박영순

Introduction

Each unit is organized in this way!

Unit Title: Each unit is titled according to the lessons topic, and it is presented in a colloquial sentence. You can see what to learn in this lesson.

Goals: For lesson objectives, main tasks, grammar, vocabulary, pronunciation, and objectives for "culture lessons" have been provided. Before beginning your lessons, think of the lesson objectives.

Get ready: This is a warming-up part which is composed of <Look at the picture and speak>, <Listen and speak> and <Vocabulary>. Through these, you can prepare the following speaking activities.

Speak: This part provides grammar practices which are preparation steps for the real-life dialogues. You can also practice important pronunciations here.

Talk: This part contains situations that you may encounter in real-life. These activities will be a good rehearsal for you.

Korean Culture: This part provides various information on Korean culture which are related to the lesson.

Check Yourself: At the end of each lesson, there is a self-evaluation chart. You can check how well you have carried out your own study plans.

Now, the exciting Korean speaking study begins!

This book has been complied strictly for you, the user. It has been complied so that you can study on your own.
It provides study objectives and self-evaluation tests, so that you can set your own study schedule and start studying on your own. Additionally, it allows you to track your progress.

You can acquire both fluency and accuracy at the same time.
It has been organized so that you will be able to communicate well during real-life conversations. At the same time, unlike other conversation-based textbooks, this book focuses on grammar and pronunciation, and provides explanations and practice exercise relating to these.

This book provides a variety of speaking activities.
Speaking exercises, which are usually boring pattern drill practices, have been organized to be dynamic and interesting, so that you will experience an enjoyable improvement in your speaking skills.

This book is filled with useful activities and authentic dialogues.
Dialogues provided in this book are simplified for beginner level, however, they are very natural dialogues which can easily be applied to real-life situations. By just memorizing the expressions from the dialogues, you should not have any problem carrying out daily speaking activities in Korea.

Useful Korean expressions and information about Korean culture are carefully incorporated in this book.
This book provides useful and handy, basic, yet crucial Korean grammar points, pronunciation, vocabulary, expression, etc., along with interesting Korean cultural information.

It's very convenient. This book is provided with a CD that includes recorded pronunciation, main vocabulary and dialogues so that you can have confidence when speaking Korean.

Scope and Sequence

Lesson	Subject	Task	Grammar
1	Introduction I	· Greetings · Introducing oneself	· −이에요/예요 · −은/는
2	Location	· Describing the location of objects	· −에 있다/없다 · −하고 · −도
3	Purchasing	· Buying products	· −에 1 · −습니다/ㅂ니다 · −(으)세요 1
4	Introduction II	· Talking about family	· −(으)세요 2 · −지 않다
5	Weekends	· Talking about your weekend	· −았/었/였− · −에 2 · −지만
6	Appointment	· Making an appointment	· −(으)ㅂ시다 · −(으)ㄹ까요? · −에서
7	Food	· Ordering food and drink · Talking about desires · taster and	· −고 싶다 · −겠− 1 · −(으)ㄹ게요
8	Invitation	· Inviting someone out or over · Accepting and declining an invitation	· −아/어/여서 1 · −지요? · −(으)ㄹ 수 있다/없다
9	Finding your way	· Finding your way · Explaining directions	· −(으)면 · −아/어/여서 2 · −(으)로 1
10	Transportation	· Using transportation facilities and convenient facilities	· −아/어/여야 되다 · −(으)로 갈아타다

Vocabulary	Pronunciation	Culture
· Vocabulary related to greetings and introduction	· Liaison 1	· Asking age · Calling by name
· Vocabulary related to place and location	· Intonation of a statement and an interrogative sentence	· Korean culture of sitting on the floor · A house facing south
· Names of objects · Numbers · Counters	· Nasalization 1	· Korean currency
· Family, Location indicator (이, 그, 저)	· Tensification 1	· The use of '우리' · Family system
· Days of the week time · Daily activity-related vocabulary	· Aspiration	· Name of days of the week · Five days in duty
· Appointment-related expressions	· /h/-deletion	· '괜찮아요?'
· Foods and tastes	· Coda rule 1 – simple coda	· Tip · '여기요'
· Birthday and invitation-related vocabulary	· Contractions and omissions in spoken language	· Expressions of hesitation · Housewarming party
· Directions	· Nasalization 2	· Dongdaemun Market
· Transportation, train, subway stations and bus stops	· /n/-insertion	· Subway

Scope and Sequence

Lesson	Subject	Task	Grammar
11	Hobby	· Asking and answering questions about hobbies	· —고 · —아/어/여 보다
12	Items	· Describing colors and shapes · Describing, selling and buying goods	· —아/어/여 주세요 · —(으)ㄴ/는 1
13	Telephone	· Calling someone · Asking for someone	· —한테서 · —(으)ㄴ/는데요
14	Mail	· Using postal services	· —(으)ㄹ 거예요 · —(이)나
15	Appearance	· Describing appearance and clothing	· —고 있다 · —(으)ㄴ 2, —는 2
16	Bank	· Depositing, withdrawing, and exchanging money at the bank	· —아/어/여야 하다 · —(으)려고 하다
17	Illness	· Talking about symptoms · Making recommendations to someone who is sick	· (으)ㄴ 것 같다 · —는 것 같다 · —(으)ㄹ 것 같다
18	Weather	· Talking about weather	· —겠— 2 · —기 전에
19	Travel	· Making a reservation · Making travel plans	· —(으)로 2 · —(으)려면
20	Lodging	· Using lodging facilities	· —(으)면 되다 · —아/어/여 주시겠어요?

Vocabulary	Pronunciation	Culture
· Vocabulary for hobbies	· Palatalization	· Online community · Game Room
· Colors and shapes	· Tensification 2	· Address terms
· Telephone · Reservation	· Coda rule 2 – complex coda	· Mobile phone
· Post office-related vocabulary	· Tensification 3	· Express Delivery Service
· Appearance and clothing-related vocabulary	· Comparison of plain stops, fortes stops and aspirated stops	· Pointing a person · Surname (Last name)
· Vocabulary necessary at the bank	· Liaison 2	· ID cards · Foreign exchange
· Illness-related vocabulary	· Tensification 4	· A herb doctor clinic
· Season and weather-related vocabulary	· Liquid	· Four seasons
· Vocabulary related to reservations	· Intonation of a choice-questions	· Tourist information · Airport
· Vocabulary related to Using lodging facilities	· Pronunciation of '의'	· *Minbak* · *Ondol*

Contents

발간사 · 5
Introduction · 8
Scope and Sequence · 10

Lesson 01 자기소개 (Introduction I) · 16

Lesson 02 위치 (Location) · 24

Lesson 03 물건 사기 (Purchasing) · 34

Lesson 04 가족 소개 (Introduction II) · 44

Lesson 05 주말 (Weekends) · 54

Lesson 06 약속 (Appointment) · 62

Lesson 07 음식 (Food) · 72

Lesson 08 초대 (Invitation) · 82

Lesson 09 길 찾기 (Finding your way) · 90

Lesson 10 교통 (Transportation) · 100

Lesson 11 취미 (Hobby) 108

Lesson 12 물건 (Items) 118

Lesson 13 전화 (Telephone) 128

Lesson 14 우편 (Mail) 138

Lesson 15 외모 (Appearance) 146

Lesson 16 은행 (Bank) 154

Lesson 17 병 (Illness) 162

Lesson 18 날씨 (Weather) 172

Lesson 19 여행 (Travel) 180

Lesson 20 숙박 (Lodging) 190

Index 198

Lesson 01 | Introduction I
자기소개

••• Goals
- **Tasks:** Greetings, Introducing oneself
- **Grammar:** −이에요/예요
    −은/는
- **Vocabulary & Expressions:** Vocabulary related to greetings and introductions
- **Pronunciation:** Liaison 1
- **Korean Culture:** Asking age, Calling by name

>>> Get Ready

What are the people doing in the pictures?
How do you greet people in your country?

Introduction | 자기소개

••• Listen

Listen to the following conversation and repeat.

김 미 정 : 안녕하세요?

톰 스미스 : 안녕하세요?

김 미 정 : 저는 김미정이에요.

톰 스미스 : 저는 톰 스미스예요.

안녕하세요? Hi   저는 I

| >>> Korean Culture |

Age is an important aspect in Korean society. When two Koreans meet for the first time, they ask each other about their age. Since Koreans regularly address each other by their appellations depending on their ages, it is especially important for Koreans to know who is older among them and address elders using appropriate titles.

017

••• Vocabulary

Vocabulary plays an important role in speaking fluent Korean. Check out the following words.

Introduction | 자기소개

>>> Speak

••• Grammar

Grammar is also an important factor in speaking Korean fluently. Look at the following grammar points.

1. **-이에요/예요**

    Copular '-이다' is attached to a noun and functions like 'be' in English. If the previous noun ends in a consonant, '-이에요' follows. If the previous noun ends in a vowel, '-예요' follows.

    > 예문 저는 학생이에요. I am a student.
    >
    > 저는 요리사예요. I am a cook.
    >
    > 저는 의사예요. I am a doctor.

2. **-은/는**

    '-은/는' is attached to a noun either when there is connotation of contrast with another subject or to indicate the topic which the speaker is intending to talk about. '-은/는' in this lesson is the topic marker. If the previous noun ends in a consonant, '-은' follows. If the previous noun ends in a vowel, '-는' follows.

    > 예문 시몽은 프랑스 사람이에요. Simon is French.
    >
    > 저는 나오코입니다. I am Naoko.
    >
    > 진아 씨는 무슨 일을 하세요? What dose Jina do for a living?

Practice

Look at the picture below and practice the conversation as suggested by the following example.

보기 리아 존슨: 안녕하세요? 리아 존슨이에요.
이 영 아: 네, 안녕하세요? 이영아예요.
리아 존슨: 이영아 씨는 한국 사람이에요?
이 영 아: 네, 저는 한국 사람이에요.

| 네 yes | 한국 사람 Korean | 영국 사람 British | 러시아 사람 Russian |
| 일본 사람 Japanese | 프랑스 사람 French | 호주 사람 Austrailian | |

①

Introduction | 자기소개

••• Pronunciation

Listen and repeat.

1. 마이클이에요.
2. 한국 사람이에요.
3. 이진아예요.

| >>> Korean Culture |

In Korea, a surname is placed before a first name. In general, a person calls another by his/her full name, but among close friends or children, quite often, only their first name is used when they address each other. In formal speech, Koreans put '씨' after a person's name. However, sometimes it sounds impolite to use '씨' after the name of someone older than yourself.

>>> Talk 1

What do you say when you meet a person for the first time? Practice the conversation as the following example suggests.

이름	나라
이진영	한국
시몽 아자니	프랑스

A : 안녕하세요? 이진영이에요.
B : 안녕하세요? 저는 시몽 아자니예요.
A : 시몽 씨는 프랑스 사람이에요?
B : 네, 진영 씨는요?
A : 저는 한국 사람이에요.

>>> Talk 2

Ask your classmates about their names and professions. Complete the chart with the information from your conversation.

이름	직업
이진아	학생

 A : 성함이 어떻게 되세요?
B : 이진아예요.
A : 진아 씨는 무슨 일을 하세요?
B : 학생이에요.

성함이 어떻게 되세요? What is your name?   무슨 일을 하세요? What do you do for a living?

022

>>> Talk 3

Introduce yourself to your classmates.

> 안녕하세요?
> 저는 _____ 이에요./예요.
> _____ 사람이에요.
> _____ 이에요./예요.

> **보기** 안녕하세요?
> 저는 김수미예요.
> 저는 한국 사람이에요.
> 저는 선생님이에요.

>>> Check Yourself

Evaluate your own improvement after studying this chapter.

	Poor	Fair	Good
I can greet others in Korean.			
I can introduce myself in Korean.			

Lesson 02 | Location
위치

••• Goals

- **Tasks:** Describing the location of objects
- **Grammar:** -에 있다/없다
  -하고
  -도
- **Vocabulary & Expressions:** Vocabulary related to place and location
- **Pronunciation:** Intonation of a statement and an interrogative sentence
- **Korean Culture:** Korean culture of sitting on the floor, A house facing south

>>> Get Ready

What is in the classroom?
What is next to the window?

Location 위치

••• Listen

Listen to the following conversation and repeat.

박미선: 책상이 어디에 있어요?

이영수: 창문 옆에 있어요.

박미선: 책상 위에 뭐가 있어요?

이영수: 공책하고 시계가 있어요.

책상 desk	창문 window	공책 notebook	시계 clock	옷장 clothes chest
어디 where	하고 and	침대 bed	있다 to be there, to exist	

>>> Korean Culture

Koreans take off their shoes when they enter a house. This custom is due to a Korean traditional living style. Koreans usually sit on the floor at home unlike Westerners who sit on a chair. Despite westernization of living style, this custom has continued in Korea until today.

025

••• Vocabulary

Vocabulary plays an important role in speaking fluent Korean. Check out the following words.

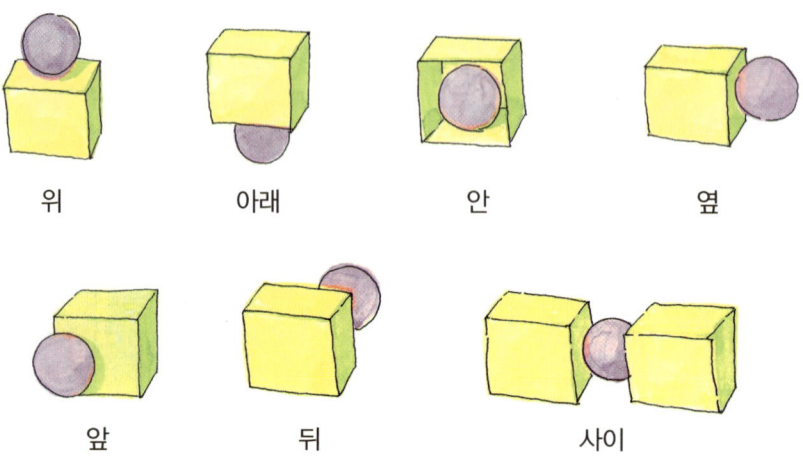

Location 위치

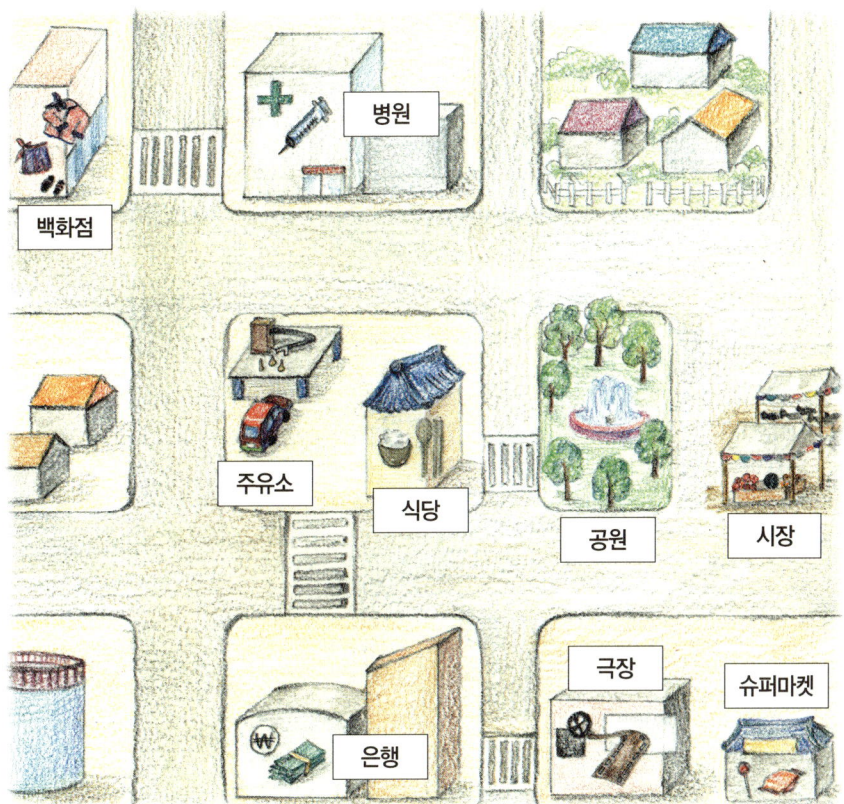

>>> Speak

••• Grammar

Grammar is also an important factor in speaking Korean fluently. Look at the following grammar points.

1. -에 있다/없다

'-에 있다' is a combination of the place particle '-에' and the verb '있다 (to exist)/없다 (not to exist)'. We use this pattern when talking about the existence or non-existence of something or someone.

예문 책상 위에 책이 있어요. There is a book on the desk.

우리 집은 은행 뒤에 있어요. My house is just behind the bank.

지금 동생이 집에 없어요.
My younger brother (or sister) is not at home right now.

교실에 지도가 없어요. There is no map in my classroom.

2. -하고

'-하고' is a particle linking two or more nouns just like 'and' in English.

예문 방에 침대하고 옷장이 있어요. The room has a bed and a chest.

거실에 피아노하고 소파가 있어요.
There are a piano and a sofa in the living room.

부엌에 식탁하고 의자가 있어요.
There are a table and chairs in the dining room.

3. -도

'-도' is translated as 'also' or 'too.'

예문 방에 책상이 있어요. 의자도 있어요.
There is a desk in the room, and a chair too.

과일을 사요. 우유도 사요.
I am buying some fruits, and a bottle of milk too.

빵을 먹어요. 콜라도 먹어요.
I am eating some bread. I am also drinking some coke.

••• Practice

Look at the picture below and practice the conversation as suggested by the following example.

Location 위치

보기
A : 방에 뭐가 있어요?
B : 방에 책상이 있어요.
   의자하고 책장도 있어요.

방

①

식당

②

사무실

컴퓨터 computer   전화 telephone   냉장고 refrigerator   식탁 dinner table   전자레인지 microwave

••• Pronunciation

Listen and repeat.

1. 안녕하세요?
2. 안녕히 계세요.
3. 책상이 있어요?
4. 네, 있어요.

029

>>> Talk 1

Choose one picture between picture A and B. In the box below check what kinds of objects there are in the picture of your choice.

Ⓐ  Ⓑ

☐ 탁자 table	☐ 그림 picture	☐ 화분 plant
☐ 커피 잔 coffee cup	☐ 컴퓨터 computer	☐ 책 book
☐ 연필 pencil	☐ 사진 photo (frame)	☐ 스탠드 desk lamp
☐ 전화 telephone		

What kinds of objects are not there? Talk about it with your partner as the following example suggests.

> 보기
> A : 탁자가 어디에 있어요?
> B : 소파 앞에 있어요.
> A : 그림이 어디에 있어요?
> B : 창문 옆에 있어요.

Location 위치

>>> Talk 2

Where is your apartment in the picture below? Describe the location of buildings as the following example suggests.

> 보기 우리 집은 은행 뒤에 있어요.
> 은행 옆에 병원이 있어요.
> 집 앞에 큰 슈퍼마켓이 있어요.

은행 bank   병원 hospital   슈퍼마켓 supermarket

>>> Korean Culture

Traditional Korean houses faced south. The house that opens to the south is cooler in summer, and warmer in winter than other types of houses. This traditional design of Korean houses is an example of scientific ingenuity of ancient Koreans.

>>> Talk 3

What does your room look like? Draw your own room and describe it.

Location 위치

제 방에 _____ 이/가 있어요.
_____ 하고 _____ 도 있어요.
_____ 앞에 _____ 이/가 있어요.
_____ 은/는 _____ 에 있어요.

보기 제 방에 책상이 있어요.
침대하고 컴퓨터도 있어요.
컴퓨터 앞에 전화가 있어요.
전화는 책상 위에 있어요.

>>> **Check Yourself**

Evaluate your own improvement after studying this chapter.

	Poor	Fair	Good
I can explain what is in a room.			
I can tell where something is in a room.			

Lesson 03 | Purchasing
물건 사기

••• Goals

- **Tasks:** Buying products
- **Grammar:** -에 1
  -습니다/ㅂ니다
  -(으)세요 1
- **Vocabulary & Expressions:** Names of products, Numbers, Counters
- **Pronunciation:** Nasalization 1
- **Korean Culture:** Korean currency

>>> Get Ready

Where do you buy the fruits?
What do they sell?

034

Purchasing 물건사기

••• Listen

Listen to the following conversation and repeat.

점 원: 어서 오세요.
조영민: 이 라면 얼마예요?
점 원: 한 개에 500원이에요.
조영민: 라면 두 개 주세요.
점 원: 모두 1,000원입니다.

점원 clerk   얼마 how much   라면 noodles   주다 to give   어서 오세요. welcome.
모두 all

| >>> Korean Culture |

There are four types of coins (10 won, 50 won, 100 won and 500 won) and three kinds of notes (1,000 won, 5,000 won and 10,000 won) in Korea. Nowadays, people also use credit cards. The official currency in Korea is 'won(KRW)'.

••• Vocabulary

Vocabulary plays an important role in speaking fluent Korean. Check out the following words.

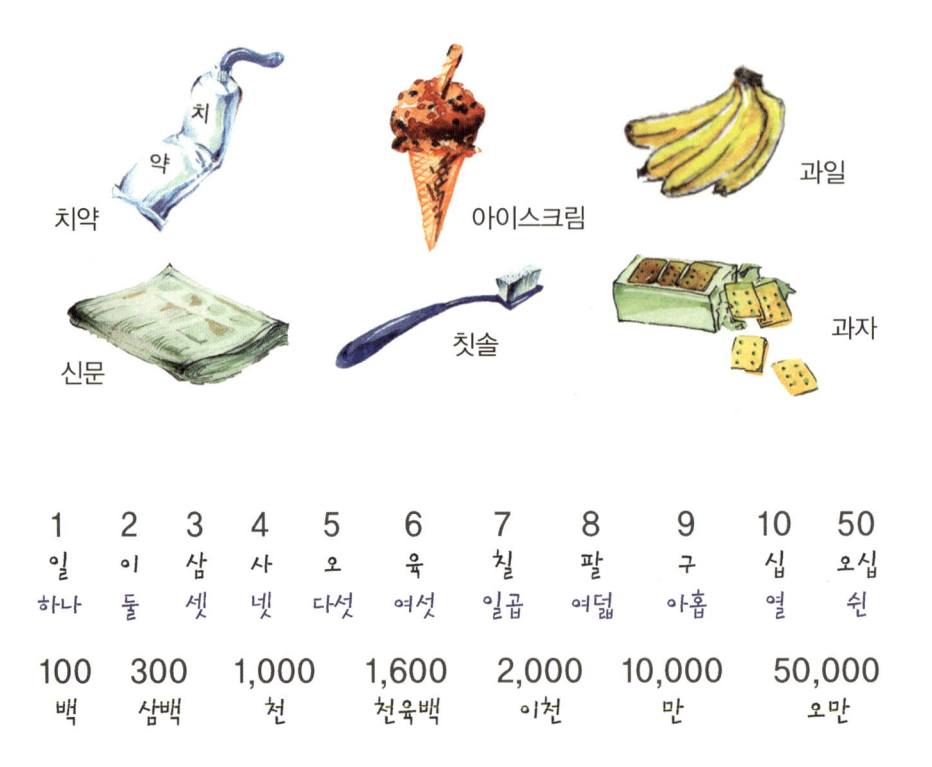

치약

아이스크림

과일

신문

칫솔

과자

1	2	3	4	5	6	7	8	9	10	50
일	이	삼	사	오	육	칠	팔	구	십	오십
하나	둘	셋	넷	다섯	여섯	일곱	여덟	아홉	열	쉰

100	300	1,000	1,600	2,000	10,000	50,000
백	삼백	천	천육백	이천	만	오만

There are two number systems in Korean. We have a pure Korean number system, which is used for smaller, more common numbers. It is the system beginning with "하나, 둘, 셋." We also have the Sino-Korean system, which is used most commonly for larger numbers. This system begins with "일, 이, 삼."

Purchasing 물건사기

병　개　권　장　대　마리　켤레

한 개　두 개　세 개　네 개　다섯 개

>>> **Speak**

••• **Grammar**

Grammar is also an important factor in speaking Korean fluently. Look at the following grammar points.

1. –에 1

   This '–에' is attached to a counting unit (such as 한 개 or 두 병) and describes the unit of measurement. For instance, '천 원에' means one thousand won is the unit of measurement, and '두 병에' means two bottls are.

   예문 천 원에 세 개입니다.
   One thousand won for three.

   맥주 두 병에 삼천 원이에요.
   Three thousand won for two bottles of beer.

   사과 한 개에 얼마예요?
   How much is an apple?

2. -습니다/ㅂ니다

'-습니다/ㅂ니다' is the formal polite form sentence ending of present tense. '-습니다' is attached to the verb or adjective stem ending in a consonant, and '-ㅂ니다' is attached to the stem ending in a vowel.

> **예문** 과일을 먹습니다. I am having some fruit.
>
> 가게에서 수박을 팝니다. The store sells watermelons.
>
> 지금 저는 한국에서 공부합니다. I am studying in Korea now.

3. -(으)세요 1

We use '-(으)세요' when making a request or giving a command. '-으세요' is attached to the verb stem ending in a consonant, and '-세요' is attached to the verb stem ending in a vowel.

> **예문** 여기 앉으세요. Please have a seat.
>
> 여기 세워 주세요. Please stop here.
>
> 잠깐만 기다려 주세요. Wait a moment, please.

••• Practice

Look at the picture below and practice the conversation as suggested by the following example.

우유
(1,500원, 1개)

빵
(2,500원, 2개)

보기

A : 어서 오세요.
B : 이 우유 얼마예요?
A : 한 개에 1,500원이에요.
B : 우유 두 개 주세요.
A : 3,000원입니다.

Purchasing 물건사기

①
아이스크림
(500원, 4개)

물
(600원, 1병)

②
라면
(700원, 5개)

사과
(1,200원, 3개)

우유 milk   빵 bread

••• Pronunciation

Listen and repeat.

1. 얼마입니까?
2. 갑니다
3. 십만 원

>>> Talk 1

You want to buy something from a grocery store. Ask the shop assistant the price of each item as the following example suggests.

- 사과 1,000원
- 치약 2,100원
- 칫솔 1,500원
- 양말 2,500원
- 잡지 7,000원

039

보기 A : 어서 오세요.
B : 사과 있어요?
A : 네, 여기 있어요.
B : 얼마예요?
A : 1,000원이에요.
B : 4개 주세요.

양말 socks   잡지 magazine

>>> Talk 2

You want to buy something from a shop. Fill in the blanks with the items you need and practice the conversation as the following example suggests.

① 편의점

② 옷가게

Purchasing **물건사기**

③ 문방구

④ 시장

장소	산 물건	가격	갯수	합계
편의점	사과 라면	800원 700원	2개 3개	3,700원
옷가게				
문방구				
시장				

보기
A : 사과 한 개에 얼마예요?
B : 한 개에 800원이에요.
A : 라면은요?
B : 한 개에 700원이에요.
A : 사과 두 개하고 라면 세 개 주세요.
B : 3,700원입니다.

>>> Talk 3

You are a shop assistant in the shops below. Advertise the items you sell as the following example suggests.

서점

옷 가게

과일 가게

신발 가게

Purchasing 물건사기

우리 가게는 _____이에요/예요.

____하고 _____이/가 있어요.

____은/는 _____에 _____원이에요.

____은/는 _____에 _____원이에요.

보기
1. 우리 가게는 서점이에요.
2. 교과서하고 사전이 있어요.
3. 교과서는 한 권에 만 오천 원이에요.
4. 사전은 한 권에 이만 원이에요.

교과서 textbook   사전 dictionary

>>> Check Yourself

Evaluate your own improvement after studying this chapter.

	Poor	Fair	Good
I can explain the products in the store.			
I can buy products using Korean.			

043

Lesson 04 | Introduction II
가족 소개

••• Goals

- **Tasks:** Talking about family
- **Grammar:** -(으)세요 2
  -지 않다
- **Vocabulary & Expressions:** Family, Location indicator (이, 그, 저)
- **Pronunciation:** Tensification 1
- **Korean Culture:** The use of '우리', Family system

>>> Get Ready

How many people are there in your family?
Where does your family live?

Introduction II **가족소개**

••• Listen

Listen to the following conversation and repeat.

톰 스미스 : 이 사진이 영민 씨 가족 사진이에요?
조 영 민 : 네. 우리 가족은 아버지, 어머니, 동생, 저 이렇게 네 명이에요.
톰 스미스 : 어머니는 직장에 다니세요?
조 영 민 : 아니요, 어머니는 직장에 다니시지 않아요.

우리 our	가족 family	이렇게 like this	직장 workplace
아니요. no.	다니다 to commute, to work		

| >>> Korean Culture |

In many cases, Korean use the word 'we' instead of 'I'. When they introduce or talk about their own family to other people, for example, they say 'our father' in place of 'my father'. The word 'we' shows the community spirit and the idea of harmony that Koreans keep in their minds.

••• Vocabulary

Vocabulary plays an important role in speaking fluent Korean. Check out the following words.

이 책은 재미있습니다.

이

그 가방이 예뻐요.

고마워요.

그

저 시계가 얼마예요?

이만 원이에요.

저

Introduction II 가족소개

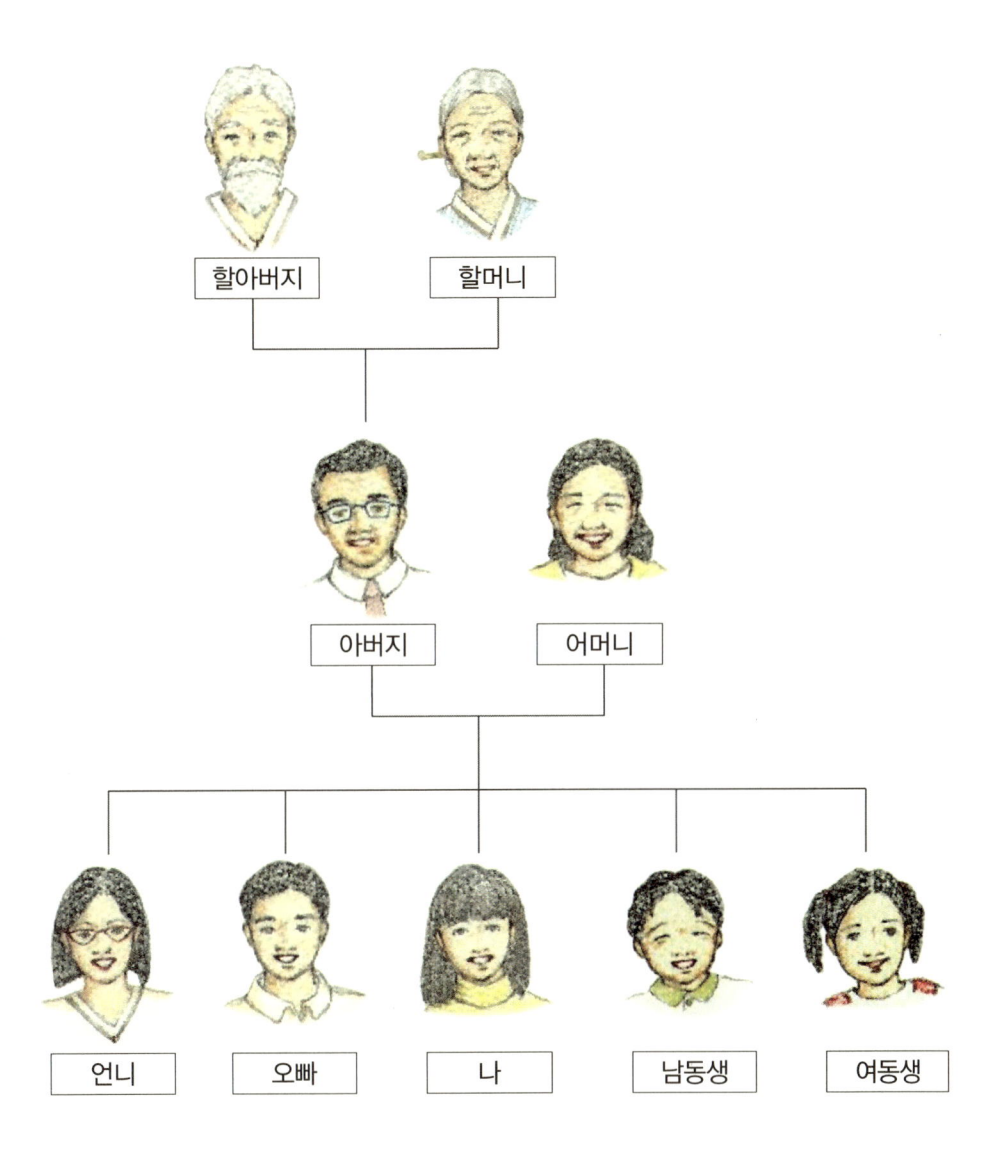

할아버지   할머니

아버지   어머니

언니   오빠   나   남동생   여동생

| >>> Korean Culture |

In the past, most of the Korean households were an 'extended family', which consists of old parents, their first son and his wife. In these days, most households are in the form of the 'nuclear family', in which a married couple is the center of a family.

047

>>> Speak

●●● Grammar

Grammar is also an important factor in speaking Korean fluently. Look at the following grammar points.

1. -(으)세요 2

This form is a combination of a honorific '-시-' and an informal sentence ending '-어요.' You can use this form to show your respect for the subject of the sentence when you describe the action or condition of the subject.

> 예문 아버지는 회사원이세요.
> My father works at an office.
>
> 어머니도 직장에 다니세요.
> My mother also has a job.
>
> 할머니께서는 시골에 사세요.
> My grandmother lives in the countryside.

2. -지 않다

This pattern, attached to the verb or adjective stem, makes a negation.

> 예문 오늘은 날씨가 좋지 않아요.
> The weather is not fine today.
>
> 제 동생은 도서관에서 공부하지 않아요.
> My younger brother doesn't study in the library.
>
> 저는 백화점에서 물건을 사지 않아요.
> I don't buy things at the department store.

Introduction II **가족소개**

••• Practice

Look at the picture below and practice the conversation as suggested by the following example.

가족 : 토니, 부인, 딸
직업 : 토니-회사원,
　　　 부인-주부

토니

보기　A : 이 사진이 토니 씨 가족 사진이에요?
　　　B : 네. 우리 가족은 아내, 저, 딸 이렇게
　　　　　세 명이에요.
　　　A : 부인은 회사에 다니세요?
　　　B : 아니요, 아내는 주부예요.

①

가족 : 할아버지, 할머니
　　　 부모님, 언니
　　　 오빠, 여동생, 마사코

직업 : 아버지-은행원
　　　 언니-변호사
　　　 오빠-의사

마사코

②

가족 : 부모님, 부인, 남동생,
　　　여동생, 딸, 미겔

직업 : 남동생-경찰
　　　여동생-학생

미겔

회사 company   은행원 banker   변호사 lawyer   경찰 police

••• Pronunciation

Listen and repeat.

1. 식당
2. 잡지
3. 비빔밥

>>> Talk 1

Talk about your family in class as the following example suggests.

이름	가족	직업
제인	아버지	회사원
	어머니	회사원
	동생	학생

Introduction II **가족소개**

이름	가족	직업

보기
A : 제인 씨 가족은 몇 명이에요?
B : 네 명이에요. 아버지, 어머니, 동생, 그리고 저예요.
A : 아버지는 은행에 다니세요?
B : 아니요. 아버지는 회사에 다니세요.
A : 어머니는요?
B : 어머니도 회사에 다니세요.

>>> Talk 2

Work with a partner. Look at the family photo below and talk about your own family to each other as the following example suggests.

보기

A : 이 사진은 누구 사진이에요?
B : 우리 가족 사진이에요.
A : 아, 그래요? 이 사람이 부인이에요?
B : 네, 그래요.
A : 부인은 회사에 다니세요?
B : 아니요. 회사에 다니지 않아요.

>>> Talk 3

Introduce your partner's family to other classmates as the following example suggests.

보기
1. 제인 씨 가족은 모두 네 명이에요.
2. 제인 씨는 아버지, 어머니, 그리고 오빠가 있어요.

3. 아버지는 회사에 다니세요.
4. 어머니도 회사원이세요.
5. 제인 씨 오빠는 학생이에요.

>>> Check Yourself

Evaluate your own improvement after studying this chapter.

	Poor	Fair	Good
I can tell others about my family.			
I can introduce my freind's family to others.			

Lesson 05 | Weekends 주말

••• Goals
- **Tasks:** Talking about your weekend
- **Grammar:** -았/었/였-
  -에 2
  -지만
- **Vocabulary & Expressions:** Days of the week time, and daily activity-related vocabulary
- **Pronunciation:** Aspiration
- **Korean Culture:** Name of days of the week, Five days in duty

>>> Get Ready

What did you do last weekend?
What do you usually do on the weekends?

Weekends 주말

••• Listen

Listen to the following conversation and repeat.

김미정 : 주말에 뭐 했어요?

이영수 : 친구하고 저녁을 먹었어요. 미정 씨는요?

김미정 : 저는 태권도를 배웠어요.

이영수 : 태권도가 재미있어요?

김미정 : 네, 어렵지만 재미있어요.

| 친구 friend | 저녁 dinner | 먹다 to eat | 태권도 Taekwondo | 배우다 to learn |
| 재미있다 to be fun, to be enjoyable, to be interesting | | | 요즘 thesedays, lately | 어렵다 to be difficult |

••• Vocabulary

Vocabulary plays an important role in speaking fluent Korean. Check out the following words.

055

월요일 Monday	화요일 Tuesday	수요일 Wednesday	목요일 Thursday	금요일 Friday	토요일 Saturday	일요일 Sunday
1	2	3	4	5	6	7
8	9	10	11	12	13	14

└ 주말 ┘

세 시 삼십 분   한 시 십오 분   다섯 시 사십 분   아홉 시 십 분

| >>> Korean Culture |

Each day in a week represents one of the seven elements of the universe including the sun and the moon. 일요일 (Sunday) means the sun; 월요일 (Monday), the moon; 화요일 (Tuesday), fire; 수요일 (Wednesday), water; 목요일 (Thursday), tree; 금요일 (Friday), metal; and 토요일 (Saturday), earth.

>>> Speak

••• Grammar

Grammar is also an important factor in speaking Korean fluently. Look at the following grammar points.

1. 았/었/였-

'-았/었/였-' is used to construct the past tense of the verbs and adjectives. When the final vowel of the verb or adjective stem is 'ㅏ' or 'ㅗ', it takes '-았-'. When the final vowel of the verb or adjective stem is other than 'ㅏ' or

'ㅗ', it takes '-었-'. When conbined with the verbs or adjectives ending with '하다', it makes either '하였어요' or '하였습니다' or '했어요' or '했습니다'. In spoken Korean, '했어요' or '했습니다' is more often used.

> **예문** 친구하고 식당에 갔어요. I went to the restaurant with my friend.
>
> 불고기를 먹었어요. I ate Bulgogi.
>
> 월요일에 뭐 했어요? What did you do on Monday?

2. -에 2

'-에' is attached to a noun indicating time and is translated as 'at,' 'an' or 'an' in English. This '-에' cannot come after adverbs, which makes such combinations as '내일에' inappropriate.

> **예문** 1시에 식사를 합니다. I have lunch at one o'lock.
>
> 오늘 저녁에 만나요. See you in the evening.
>
> 주말에 영화를 봤어요. I watched a movie last weekend.

3. -지만

'-지만' is attached to the verb or adjective stem, and connects two sentences which are in contrast with each other similar to 'but' in English.

> **예문** 한국말 공부는 어렵지만 재미있어요.
> Studying Korean is difficult but interesting.
>
> 토요일에는 수업이 없지만 학교에 갑니다.
> There is no class on Saturdays but I go to school.
>
> 점심을 먹었지만 배가 고파요. I had lunch but I still feel hungry.

••• Practice

Look at the picture below and practice the conversation as suggested by the following example.

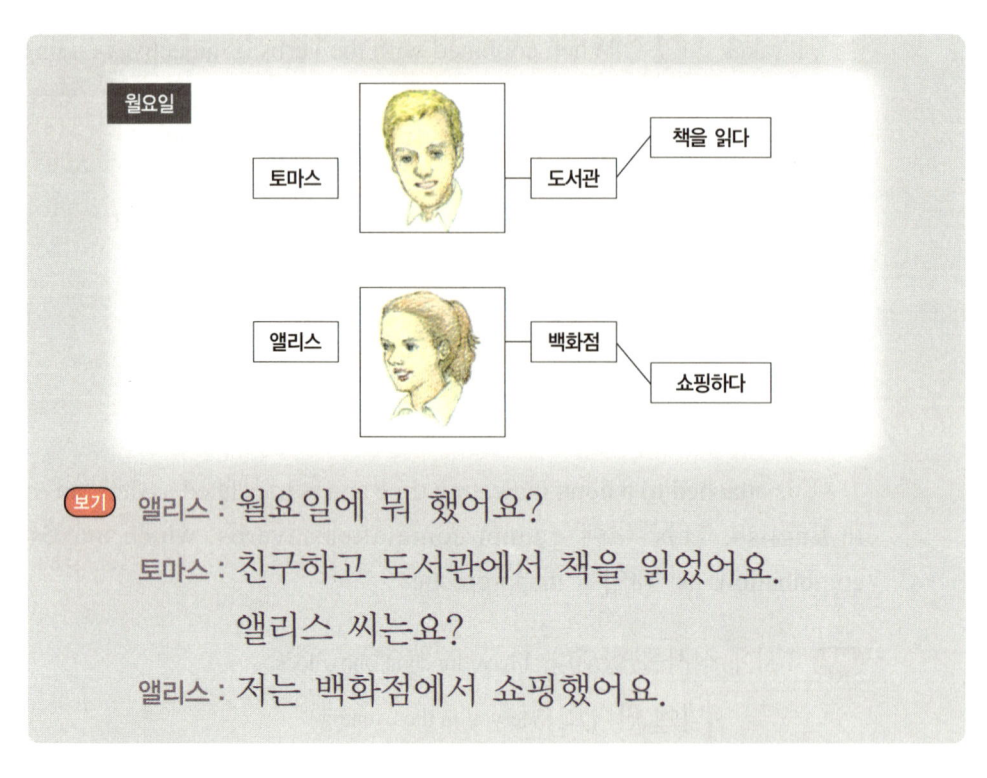

|보기| 앨리스: 월요일에 뭐 했어요?
토마스: 친구하고 도서관에서 책을 읽었어요.
앨리스 씨는요?
앨리스: 저는 백화점에서 쇼핑했어요.

① 수요일

마이클 — 노래방 — 노래를 부르다

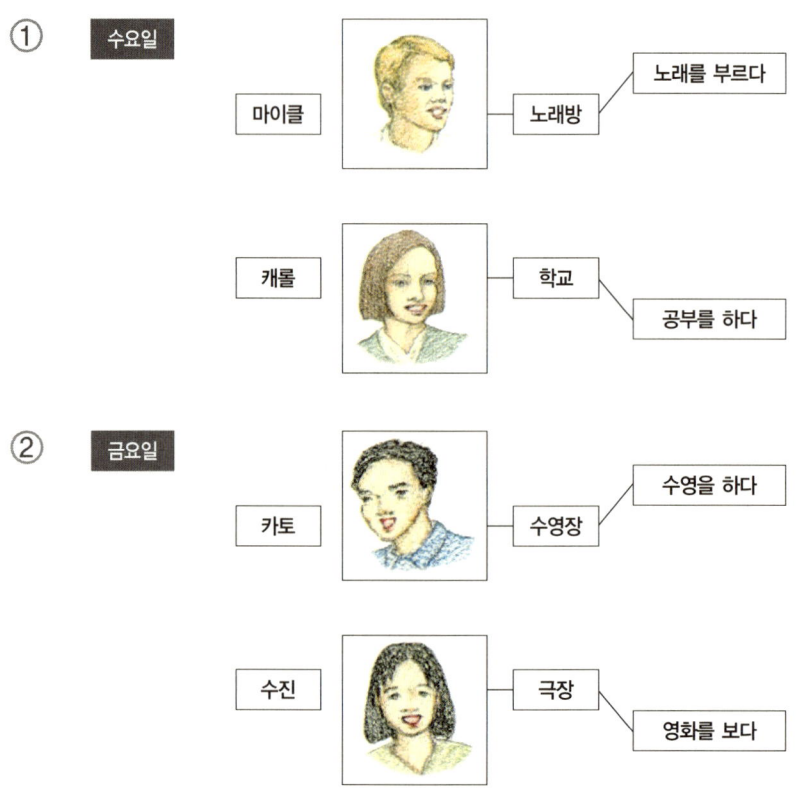

캐롤 — 학교 — 공부를 하다

② 금요일

카토 — 수영장 — 수영을 하다

수진 — 극장 — 영화를 보다

Weekends 주말

도서관 library	책 book	읽다 to read	쇼핑 shopping	노래방 *Noraebang*
노래를 부르다 to sing	학교 school	수영장 swimming pool		수영을 하다 to swim
영화관 movie theater	영화를 보다 to watch a movie			

••• Pronunciation

Listen and repeat.

1. 많다
2. 좋다
3. 이렇게
4. 그렇지만

>>> Talk 1

What did you do last Saturday? Talk about it as the following example suggests.

보기

A : 토요일에 뭐 했어요?
B : 영화관에 갔어요.
　　영화를 봤어요.
A : 재미있었어요?
B : 네, 재미있었어요.

영화관

① 수영장　　　② 공원

공원 park　　　산책을 하다 to take a walk

>>> Korean Culture

Since 2002, major banks and companies in Korea have started introducing a 'five day workweek system'. Today, more and more companies are implementing this system. As a result, people can have more free time for trips and shopping, since the weekend starts from a Friday evening. Even new movies are now released on Fridays instead of Saturdays, which attracts people to enjoy their early weekends.

>>> Talk 2

What did you do last weekend? Talk about it as the following example suggests.

보기
저는 지난 주말에 친구를 만났어요.
친구와 공원에 갔어요.
산책을 했어요.
책도 읽었어요.
재미있었어요.

Weekends 주말

>>> Talk 3

What did you do on weekends in your country? Talk about it as the following example suggests.

> **보기** 저는 주말에 회사에 가지 않았어요.
> 집에서 쉬었어요.
> 친구들도 만났어요.
> 여행도 했어요.
> 즐겁게 지냈어요.

친구를 만나다 to meet freinds   즐겁게 지내다 to have a good time

>>> Check Yourself

Evaluate your own improvement after studying this chapter.

	Poor	Fair	Good
I can talk about what I did on weekends with friends.			
I can talk about what people in my country usually do on weekends.			

061

Lesson 06 | Appointment
약속

••• Goals

- **Tasks:** Making an appointment
- **Grammar:** -(으)ㅂ시다
  -(으)ㄹ까요?
  -에서
- **Vocabulary & Expressions:** Appointment-related expressions
- **Pronunciation:** /h/-deletion
- **Korean Culture:** '괜찮아요?'

>>> Get Ready

What time are they meeting?
Where are they meeting?

Appointment 약속

••• Listen

Listen to the following conversation and repeat.

박미선: 주말에 같이 영화 볼까요?
김미정: 네, 좋아요. 몇 시에 만날까요?
박미선: 세 시쯤 괜찮아요?
김미정: 좋아요. 어디에서 만날까요?
박미선: 영화관 앞에서 다섯 시에 만납시다.

같이 together	영화 보다 to go to the movies	좋다 to be good	몇 what
만나다 to meet	괜찮아요? Is it okay with you?	쯤 around	

063

| >>> Korean Culture |

The expression "괜찮아요?" is usually used when people make an appointment or ask other's opinion. For example, "다섯 시 괜찮아요?" or "비빔밥 괜찮아요?"

••• Vocabulary

Vocabulary plays an important role in speaking fluent Korean. Check out the following words.

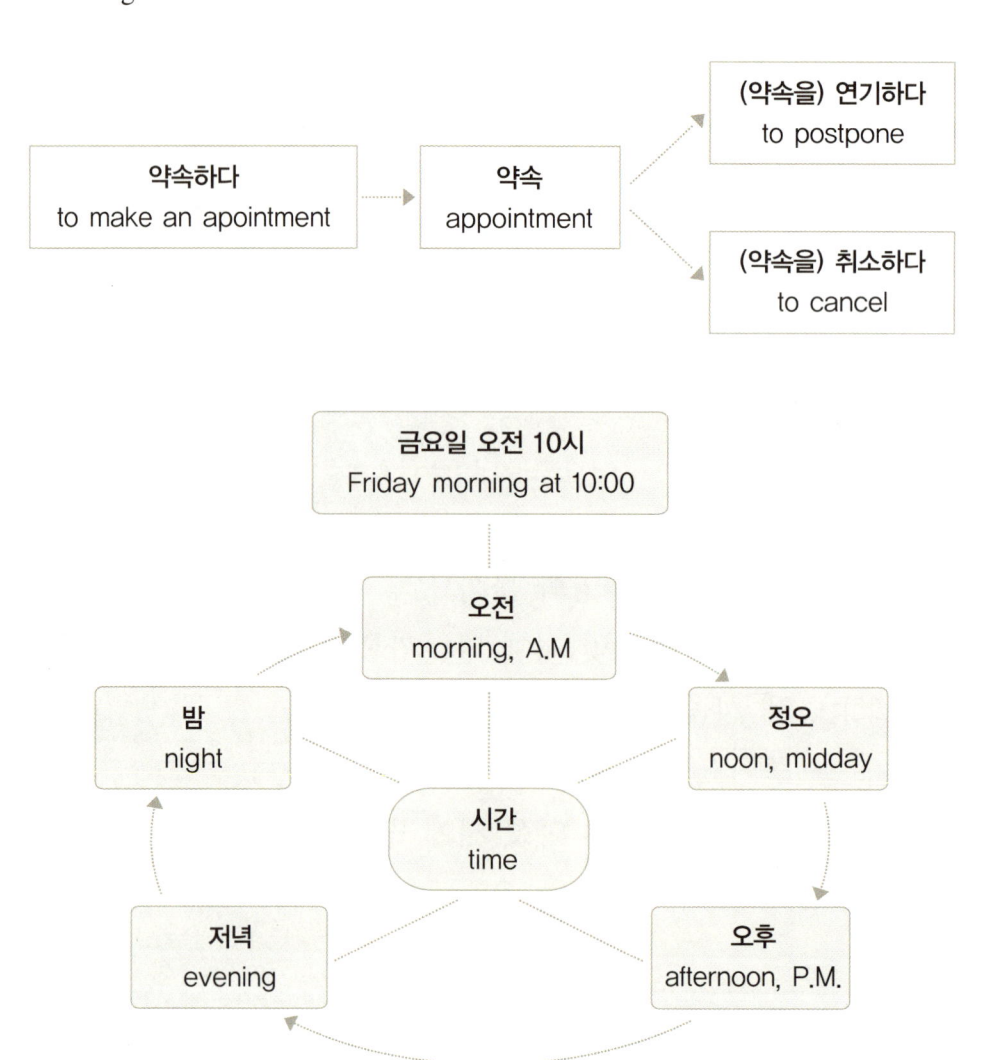

약속하다 — to make an apointment

약속 — appointment

(약속을) 연기하다 — to postpone

(약속을) 취소하다 — to cancel

금요일 오전 10시
Friday morning at 10:00

오전 — morning, A.M
정오 — noon, midday
오후 — afternoon, P.M.
저녁 — evening
밤 — night
시간 — time

Appointment 약속

> **Speak**

Grammar

Grammar is also an important factor in speaking Korean fluently. Look at the following grammar points.

1. -(으)ㅂ시다

You can use this form when you propose or suggest something to the listener. '-읍시다' is attached to the verb stem ending in a consonant, and '-ㅂ시다' is attached to the verb stem ending in a vowel.

> 예문 저녁을 함께 먹읍시다. Let's have dinner together.
>
> 우리 같이 갑시다. Let's go together.
>
> 주말에 영화를 봅시다. Let's watch a movie this weekend.

2. -(으)ㄹ까요?

In spoken Korean, '-(으)ㄹ까요?' is used to make a suggestion or inquire about someone's inclination. The subject of the sentence '우리 (we)' is often omitted. Since '-(으)ㄹ까요?' takes the form of the question, it sounds softer or politer than '-(으)ㅂ시다' when making a suggestion. '-을까요?' is attached to the verb stem ending in a consonant, and '-ㄹ까요?' is attached to the verb stem ending in a vowel.

> 예문 같이 점심을 먹을까요? How about having lunch together?
>
> 우리 이야기 좀 할까요? Let's talk for a moment.
>
> 언제 만날까요? When shall we meet?

3. –에서

'–에서' is attached to a place noun to indicate the place where an action occurs (or occurred). It is usually followed by the verbs such as '먹다', '자다', '살다' and '만나다' the meaning of which does not have the change of places like '오다' and '가다'.

> (예문) 공원에서 책을 읽었어요. I read a book at the park.
> 기숙사에서 잠을 잤어요. I slept in my dorm room.
> 저는 서울에서 살아요. I live in Seoul.

••• Practice

Look at the picture below and practice the conversation as suggested by the following example.

금요일 오전 10시, 시청

등산 가다

(보기) A : 금요일에 같이 등산 갈까요?
B : 네, 좋아요. 몇 시에 만날까요?
A : 열 시쯤 괜찮아요?
B : 네, 어디에서 만날까요?
A : 시청 앞에서 만납시다.

Appointment 약속

① 수요일 오후 5시, 예술의 전당

공연을 보다

② 일요일 오전 11시, 한국백화점

백화점에서 쇼핑하다

등산 가다 to go hiking to a mountain   공연을 보다 to watch a performance

••• Pronunciation

Listen and repeat.

1. 좋아요.
2. 많아요.
3. 괜찮아요.

067

>>> Talk 1

Look at the posters below and make an appointment with your partner as the following example suggests.

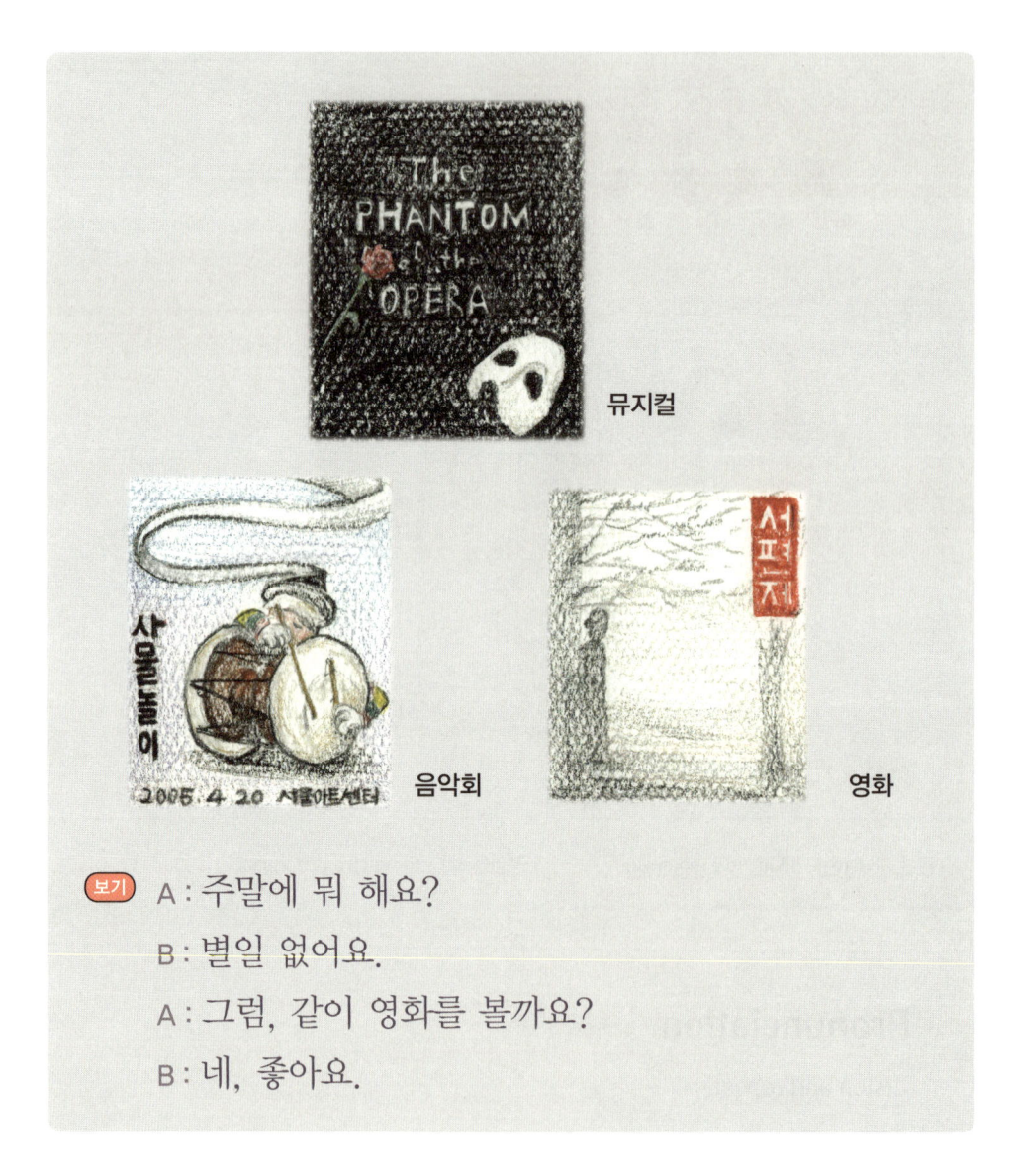

뮤지컬

음악회

영화

보기
A : 주말에 뭐 해요?
B : 별일 없어요.
A : 그럼, 같이 영화를 볼까요?
B : 네, 좋아요.

별일 없다 to have nothing special   그럼 then

Appointment 약속

>>> Talk 2

Talk with your partner and set a time that you will meet later.

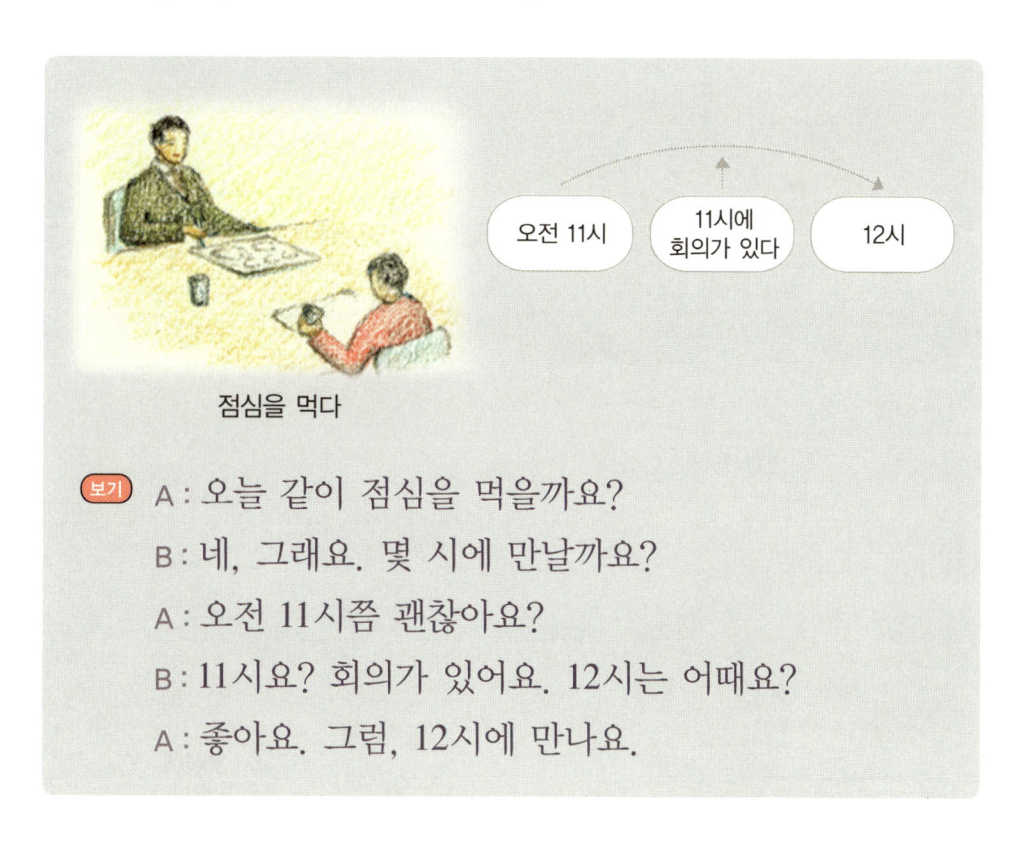

오전 11시 → 11시에 회의가 있다 → 12시

점심을 먹다

보기
A : 오늘 같이 점심을 먹을까요?
B : 네, 그래요. 몇 시에 만날까요?
A : 오전 11시쯤 괜찮아요?
B : 11시요? 회의가 있어요. 12시는 어때요?
A : 좋아요. 그럼, 12시에 만나요.

①

오후 5시 → 5시에 일이 있다 → 6시

산책하다

069

② 테니스 치다

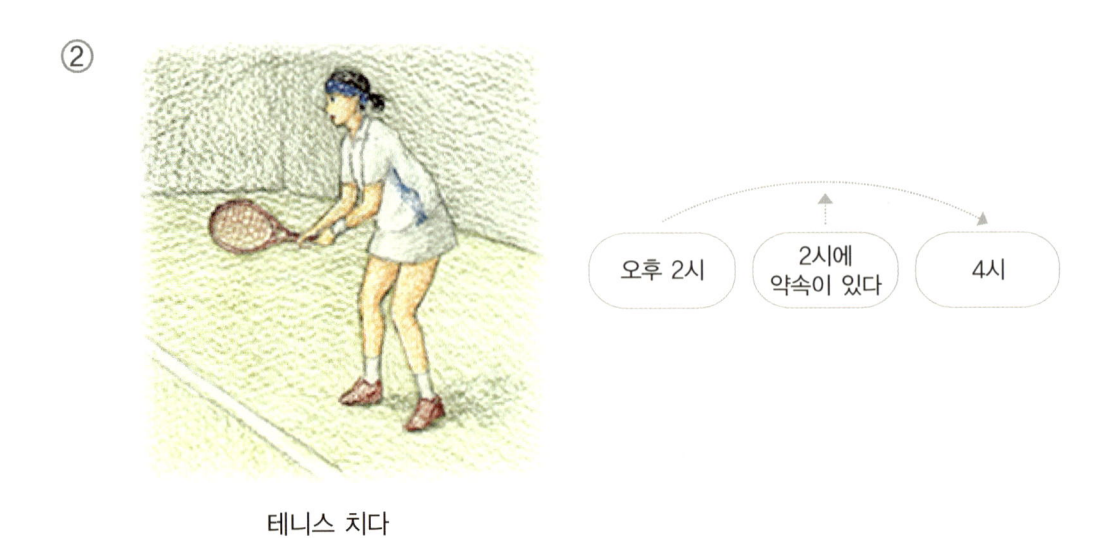

오후 2시 — 2시에 약속이 있다 — 4시

③ 도서관에서

오후 4시 — 4시 30분에 수업이 끝나다 — 5시

오늘 today   회의 meeting   테니스 치다 to play tennis

>>> Talk 3

Have you cancelled your appointments? Practice a conversation as the following example suggests.

> 보기 A : 수미 씨, 저는 토요일에 영화를 볼 수 없어요.
> B : 왜요? 무슨 일 있어요?
> A : 네, 미국에서 어머니가 오세요.
> B : 괜찮아요. 영화는 나중에 봐요.

왜 why   무슨 일 있어요? Is there any problem?   괜찮아요. That's all right.   나중에 later

>>> Check Yourself

Evaluate your own improvement after studying this chapter.

	Poor	Fair	Good
I can make appointments.			
I can cancel appointments.			

Lesson 07 | Food
음식

••• Goals
- **Tasks:** Ordering food and drink, Talking about desires and tastes
- **Grammar:** -고 싶다
  -겠- 1
  -(으)ㄹ게요
- **Vocabulary & Expressions:** Foods and tastes
- **Pronunciation:** Coda rule 1 – simple coda
- **Korean Culture:** Tip, '여기요'

>>> Get Ready

Have you ever been this place?
What is your favorite food?

Food 음식

●●● Listen

Listen to the following conversation and repeat.

박미선 : 뭘 드시겠어요?
조영민 : 전 비빔밥을 먹고 싶어요.
박미선 : 비빔밥요?
조영민 : 네, 미선 씨는 뭘 드시겠어요?
박미선 : 전 불고기를 시킬게요.

| 뭘 what | 들다 to eat | 전 I | 시키다 to order |

>>> Korean Culture

In ordinary Korean restaurants, there is no tipping system. However people give tips in hotels or some high-class restaurants to show their appreciation of superior service.

••• Vocabulary

Vocabulary plays an important role in speaking fluent Korean. Check out the following words.

맵다   짜다   달다   시다   쓰다

한식	비빔밥	냉면	불고기
양식	스파게티	스테이크	햄버거

Food 음식

일식	회	초밥	우동
중식	탕수육	만두	자장면

>>> Speak

••• Grammar

Grammar is also an important factor in speaking Korean fluently. Look at the following grammar points.

1. -고 싶다

This pattern is used to express the subject's desire or wish to do something. It is attached to the action verb stem. In statements 'I' is the subject of the sentence, and in questions 'you' is the subject of the sentence.

075

예문 아이스크림을 먹고 싶어요. I want to have some ice cream.

좀 쉬고 싶어요. I want to take a rest.

영화를 보고 싶어요? Do you want to watch a movie?

2. -겠- 1

'-겠-' is used to construct the future tense. It expresses the speaker's determination or intention in statements, and inquirines about the listener's determination or intention in questions.

예문 저는 불고기를 먹겠습니다. I will have Bulgogi.

다음 달부터 한국어를 배우겠습니다.
I will start learning Korean next month.

무엇을 드시겠습니까? What would you have?

3. -(으)ㄹ게요

'-(으)ㄹ게요' usually expresses the speaker's promise to the listener in spoken language. Sometimes it also expresses the speaker's intention or determination. Only statements with the first person subject can take this ending. '-을게요' is attached to the verb stem ending in a consonant, and '-ㄹ게요' to the verb stem ending in a vowel.

예문 내일 연락할게요. I will call you tomorrow.

내가 도와줄게요. I will help you.

난 비빔밥을 먹을게요. I will have Bibimbap.

••• Practice

Look at the picture below and practice the conversation as suggested by the following example.

Food 음식

항아리(한식집)

불고기	10,000원
갈비	15,000원
냉면	5,000원
비빔밥	5,000원
된장찌개	5,000원

보기

크리스: 뭘 드시겠어요?
마이클: 전 냉면을 먹고 싶어요.
　　　　크리스 씨는요?
크리스: 전 비빔밥을 시킬게요.
마이클: 여기요!
　　　　냉면하고 비빔밥 주세요.

① **시실리아(양식집)**

스테이크	30,000원
햄버거	20,000원
스파게티	10,000원
피자	15,000원
라자니아	10,000원

② **짱아네(분식집)**

라면	3,000원
쫄면	3,000원
김밥	2,000원
칼국수	4,000원
떡볶이	2,000원

>>> Korean Culture

When people call a waiter/waitress in restaurants to order or to ask for something, they say "여기요".

••• Pronunciation

Listen and repeat.

1. 부엌
2. 집 앞
3. 비옷

>>> Talk 1

Look at the desserts below. Point out your favorite and explain why.

떡 케이크 녹차 과자

식혜 홍차

수정과 커피 배 아이스크림

딸기 포도

사과 멜론

보기 나는 녹차가 좋아요.
그래서 녹차를 자주 마셔요.

그래서 so   자주 often

>>> Talk 2

Work with your partner. Discuss where you want to go for dinner with him/her.

〈한식집 '청사초롱'〉

메뉴	정식 (40,000원) 	갈비찜 (25,000원) 불고기 (20,000원) 비빔밥 (10,000원)

〈중국집 '북경'〉

메뉴	정식 (30,000원) 	자장면 (3,500원) 탕수육 (20,000원)

〈일식집 '죽원'〉

메뉴	정식 (70,000원) 	회덮밥 (20,000원) 초밥 (25,000원) 모둠회 (150,000원)

〈양식집 '웨스턴 우드'〉		
메뉴	정식 (45,000원)	스테이크 (30,000원) 스파게티 (15,000원) 샐러드 (20,000원) 수프 (8,000원)

보기
A : 어디에서 저녁 먹을까요?
B : 저는 한식이 좋아요.
A : 그럼 청사초롱에 갈까요?
B : 네, 좋아요. 그럼, 거기에서 뭘 먹을까요?
A : 정식 어때요?
B : 정식은 좀 비싸요.

정식 table d'hote   회덮밥 Hoedeopbap   모둠회 Modumhoe
샐러드 salad   수프 soup   거기 there   비싸다 to be expensive

>>> Talk 3

Introduce some of the popular foods in your country as the following example suggests.

Food 음식

한국	〈여러분 나라〉
김치 불고기 비빔밥	

> **보기** 한국에서는 김치를 많이 먹어요.
> 김치는 맛이 매워요.
> 그렇지만 건강에 좋아요.
> 우리 가족도 김치를 많이 먹어요.

김치 *Gimchi*　　그렇지만 however　　건강 health

>>> Check Yourself

Evaluate your own improvement after studying this chapter.

	Poor	Fair	Good
I can order food at a restaurant.			
I can introduce popular foods in my country.			
I can introduce the food I like.			

081

Lesson 08 | Invitation 초대

••• Goals

- **Tasks:** Inviting someone out or over, Accepting and declining an invitation
- **Grammar:** -아/어/여서 1
  -지요?
  -(으)ㄹ 수 있다/없다
- **Vocabulary & Expressions:** Birthday and invitation-related vocabulary
- **Pronunciation:** Contractions and omissions in spoken language
- **Korean Culture:** Expressions of hesitation, Housewarming party

>>> Get Ready

What is the occasion?
How do you celebrate your birthday?

Invitation 초대

••• Listen

Listen to the following conversation and repeat.

박미선: 미정 씨, 내일 저녁에 시간 있어요?

김미정: 네, 괜찮아요.

박미선: 그럼, 내일 우리 집에 올 수 있지요?
　　　　제 생일이에요.

김미정: 네, 좋아요.

박미선: 스미스 씨는 어때요?

톰스미스: 전 내일 오후에 약속이 있어요. 미안해요.

| 내일 tomorrow | 제 my | 미안해요. I'm sorry. |

083

| >>> Korean Culture |

When you turn down someone's invitation, you have to show the person your appreciation for inviting you before explaining why you are unable to attend. An outright refusal is considered rude in Korea. Koreans start their refusal with 저…(well)' or '사실은 (in fact, actually)' as expressions of hesitation. After that, they explain their situation and the reason.

••• Vocabulary

Vocabulary plays an important role in speaking fluent Korean. Check out the following words.

초대장
파티
축하 노래
생일
Birthday
케이크
꽃다발
카드
선물

>>> Speak

••• Grammar

Grammar is also an important factor in speaking Korean fluently. Look at the following grammar points.

084

Invitation 초대

1. -아/어/여서 1

'-아/어/여서' expresses a reason or a cause. When the final vowel of the verb or adjective stem is 'ㅏ' or 'ㅗ', it takes '-아서'. When the final vowel of the verb or adjective stem is other than 'ㅏ' or 'ㅗ', it takes '-어서'. When combined with the verbs or adjectives ending with '하다', it makes either '하여서' or '해서'. In spoken Korean, '해서' is more often used.

> 예문 차가 많아서 늦었습니다. I am late because there was a heavy traffic.
> 늦어서 미안합니다. I am sorry for being late.
> 피곤해서 일찍 잤어요. I went to bed early because I was tired.

2. -지요?

'-지요?' is used when the speaker wants to verify the listener's agreement with already known or assumed fact. The past tense is '-었/았/였지요?', and the future tense is '-을 거지요?'. In spoken Korean, we usually say the shortened form '-죠?'.

> 예문 거기가 3277-2891이지요?/이죠? Isn't it 3277-2891 there?
> 저녁 먹었지요?/먹었죠? You had dinner, didn't you?
> 저녁에 시간이 있지요?/있죠? You are free this evening, aren't you?

3. -(으)ㄹ 수 있다/없다

This pattern expresses ability / inability or possibility / impossibility.

> 예문 한국말로 편지를 쓸 수 있어요. I can write a letter in Korean.
> 저는 수영을 할 수 있어요. I can swim.
> 내일은 테니스를 칠 수 없어요. I cannot play tennis tomorrow.
> 오늘은 일찍 집에 갈 수 없어요. I cannot go home early today.

●●● Practice

Look at the picture below and practice the conversation as suggested by the following example.

A	B	C
1. 내일 오후, 저녁, 식사 초대	O	X
2. 토요일 저녁, 생일 파티 초대	O	X
3. 금요일 저녁, 집들이 초대	O	X

보기 A : 내일 오후에 시간 있어요?
　　　B : 괜찮아요.
　　　A : 그럼, 우리 집에 올 수 있지요?
　　　　　저녁을 같이 먹어요.
　　　B : 네, 좋아요.
　　　A : 수미 씨는요?
　　　C : 저는 오후에 수업이 있어요. 미안해요.

●●● Pronunciation

Listen and repeat.

1. 저는 → 전
2. 그러면 → 그럼
3. 그런데 → 근데
4. 무엇을 → 뭘
5. 이것 → 이거

Invitation 초대

>>> Talk 1

You plan to invite your friend over to your home this weekend. Take each calendar and practice the conversation as the following example suggests.

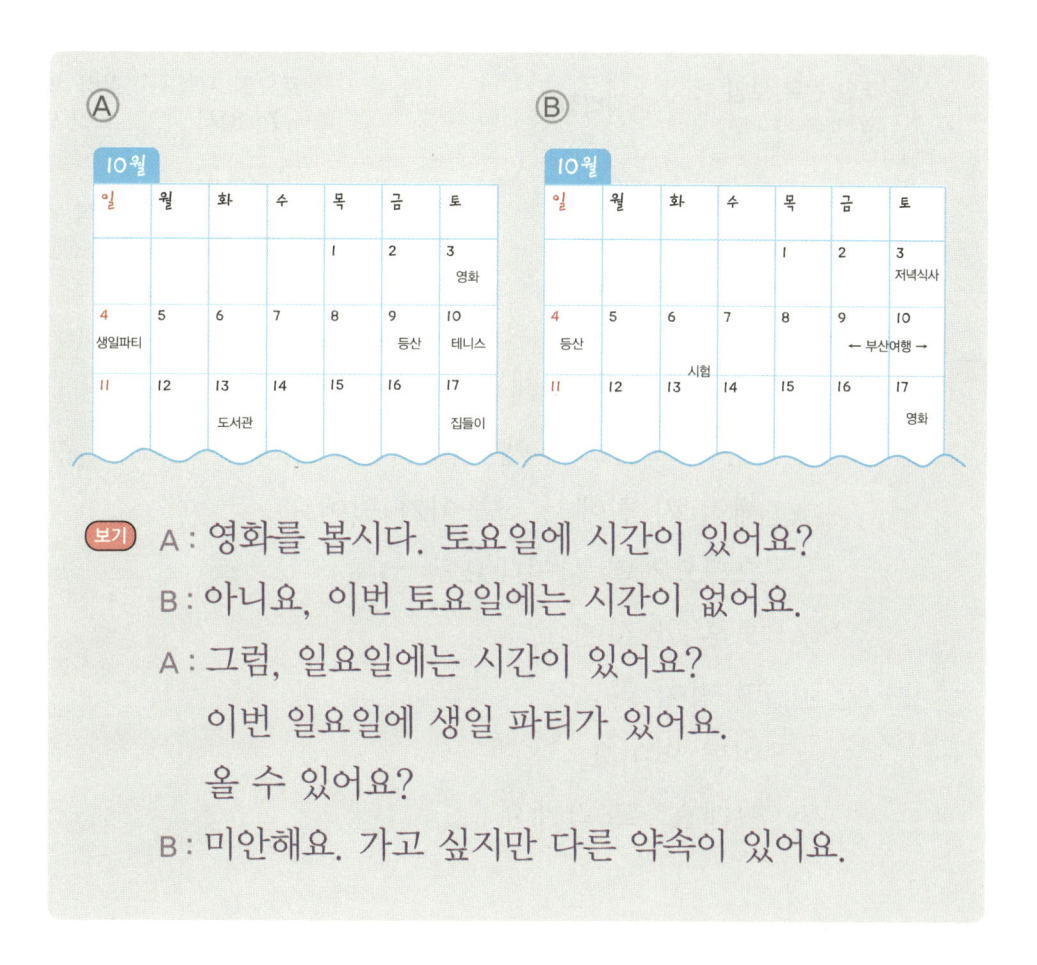

Ⓐ
10월

일	월	화	수	목	금	토
			1	2	3 영화	
4 생일파티	5	6	7	8	9	10 등산 테니스
11	12	13 도서관	14	15	16	17 집들이

Ⓑ
10월

일	월	화	수	목	금	토
			1	2	3 저녁식사	
4 등산	5	6 시험	7	8	9	10 ← 부산여행 →
11	12	13	14	15	16	17 영화

보기
A : 영화를 봅시다. 토요일에 시간이 있어요?
B : 아니요, 이번 토요일에는 시간이 없어요.
A : 그럼, 일요일에는 시간이 있어요?
 이번 일요일에 생일 파티가 있어요.
 올 수 있어요?
B : 미안해요. 가고 싶지만 다른 약속이 있어요.

>>> Talk 2

Work with your partner. Check each occasion below and take the role of an inviter, while your partner either accepts or describes your invitation as the following exemple suggests.

087

초대 내용 (occasion)	장소 (location)	인원 (number of guests)	시간 (time)	음식/기타 (food, etc.)
집들이 (house warming party)	제인 씨 집	8명	토요일 오후 1~3시	한식/ 선물 준비
주말 친목 모임 (weekend party)	갈비집	15명	토요일 저녁 7~10시	갈비, 맥주/ 회비 있음
약혼식 (engagement ceremony)	호텔	90명	금요일 저녁 7~10시	양식 뷔페/ 정장, 선물 준비

보기
A: 토요일 오후에 시간 있어요?
B: 네, 토요일 오후에 괜찮아요.
A: 제인 씨 집에서 집들이가 있어요.
B: 그래요? 몇 시인데요?
A: 오후 한 시예요.
B: 몇 명이 와요?
A: 여덟 명이요.
B: 그래요, 꼭 갈게요.

준비 preparation
약혼식 engagement ceremony
회비 membership fee, participation fee
정장 formal suit
갈비 *Galbi*
뷔페 buffet

>>> Korean Culture

'집들이 (a housewarming party)' is to invite friends or colleagues to a new house which a person moved into. People invited bring necessities for daily life such as tissues or detergents.

>>> Talk 3

What gifts do people usually bring when invited in your country? Fill the chart below and introduce them to your classmates.

생일	집들이	결혼식

결혼식 wedding ceremony

>>> Check Yourself

Evaluate your own improvement after studying this chapter.

	Poor	Fair	Good
I can invite someone over (or out).			
I can accept an invitation and politely decline an invitation.			
I can introduce the custom of bringing a gift when people are invited in my country.			

Lesson 09 | Finding your way
길 찾기

••• Goals

- **Tasks:** Finding your way; Explaining directions
- **Grammar:** -(으)면
  -아/어/여서 2
  -(으)로 1
- **Vocabulary & Expressions:** Directions
- **Pronunciation:** Nasalization 2
- **Korean Culture:** Dongdaemoon Market

>>> Get Ready

What is this woman doing?
Where does she want to go?

Finding your way 길 찾기

••• Listen

Listen to the following conversation and repeat.

톰 스미스 : 남대문시장이 어디에 있어요?
아 저 씨 : 길 건너 백화점 뒤에 있어요.
톰 스미스 : 저 백화점이요?
아 저 씨 : 네, 이 쪽으로 쭉 가면 사거리가 나와요.
거기에 횡단보도가 있어요.
횡단보도를 건너서 오른쪽으로 올라가세요.

| 건너 across | 쭉 straight | 사거리 intersaction | 올라가다 to go up |

>>> Korean Culture

'Dongdaemun Market' is the place that never sleeps. The big shopping malls and thousands of small shops open until the next morning. The market is crowded with people who enjoy shopping after midnight. Public announcement in both Japanese and English helps foreign tourists to navigate their way in the crowded marketplace.

••• Vocabulary

Vocabulary plays an important role in speaking fluent Korean. Check out the following words.

버스 정류장	bus stop	동쪽	east
		서쪽	west
횡단보도	crosswalk	남쪽	south
육교	walking overpass	북쪽	north
		오른쪽	right
지하도	walking underpass	왼쪽	left

>>> Speak

••• Grammar

Grammar is also an important factor in speaking Korean fluently. Look at the following grammar points.

1. -(으)면

'-(으)면' indicates the condition for the following sentence similar to 'if' in English. '-으면' is attached to the verb and adjective stem ending in a consonant, and '-면' is attached to the stem ending in a vowel.

> 예문 조금만 더 걸으면 됩니다. If you walk a little more, you will get there.

이 길로 쭉 가면 육교가 나와요.
If you go straight, you will see an overhead walkway.

배가 고프면 먼저 식사하세요. If you are hungry, you can eat first.

2. -아/어/여서 2

'-아/어/여서' indicates that the action in the following clause happens after, but in connection with the action of the preceding clause. It is usually used with the action verbs, and the subject of the first and second clause should be the same. What makes this form different from '-고' is that the two actions are closely related.

> 예문 은행에 가서 돈을 찾으세요. Go to the bank and withdraw some money.

횡단보도를 건너서 왼쪽으로 가세요. Cross the crosswalk and turn left.

친구를 만나서 식사를 했어요.
I met a friend of mine and had lunch together.

cf. 친구를 만나고 식사를 했어요.
I met a friend of mine and then I had lunch (either alone or with someone other than the friend I met before.)

사과를 씻어서 먹습니다. I wash an apple and eat it.

cf. 사과를 씻고 먹습니다.
I wash an apple, and eat something (other than the apple)

3. -(으)로 1

'-(으)로' indicates the direction of movement and is translated as 'to' or 'toward' in English. If the previous noun ends in a consonant, '-으로' follows. If the previous noun ends in a vowel, '-로' follows.

예문 오른쪽으로 가세요. Turn right.

이 버스는 잠실 운동장으로 갑니다. This bus heads to Jamsil Stadium.

뒤로 가서 기다리세요. Go to the back and wait.

••• Practice

Look at the picture below and practice the conversation as suggested by the following example.

Finding your way 길 찾기

한국병원, 대한은행 앞, 육교, 똑바로 올라가다

보기 A : 한국병원이 어디에 있어요?
B : 대한은행 앞에 있어요.
A : 길은 어디서 건너요?
B : 이 쪽으로 쭉 가면 사거리가 나와요.
거기에 육교가 있어요.
육교를 건너서 똑바로 올라가세요.

① 여름찻집 — 책방 뒤, 쭉 가다, 횡단보도, 오른쪽으로 돌아가다

② 가나다백화점 — 한국호텔 앞, 쭉 가다, 왼쪽으로 돌아가다, 횡단보도

나오다 to come out   똑바로 straight

••• Pronunciation

Listen and repeat.

1. 정류장
2. 종로
3. 정리해요

095

>>> Talk 1

Ask each other how to get to each place illustrated in the picture and how long it will take to get there.

보기
A : 은행이 어디에 있어요?
B : 쭉 가서 두 번째 사거리에서 왼쪽으로 가면 오른쪽에 은행이 있어요.
A : 얼마나 걸려요?
B : 한 20분쯤 걸릴 거예요.

미장원 beauty salon   얼마나 how much   걸리다 to take   한 about

Finding your way 길 찾기

>>> Talk 2

You want to go to the department store. Ask people how to get there as the following example suggests.

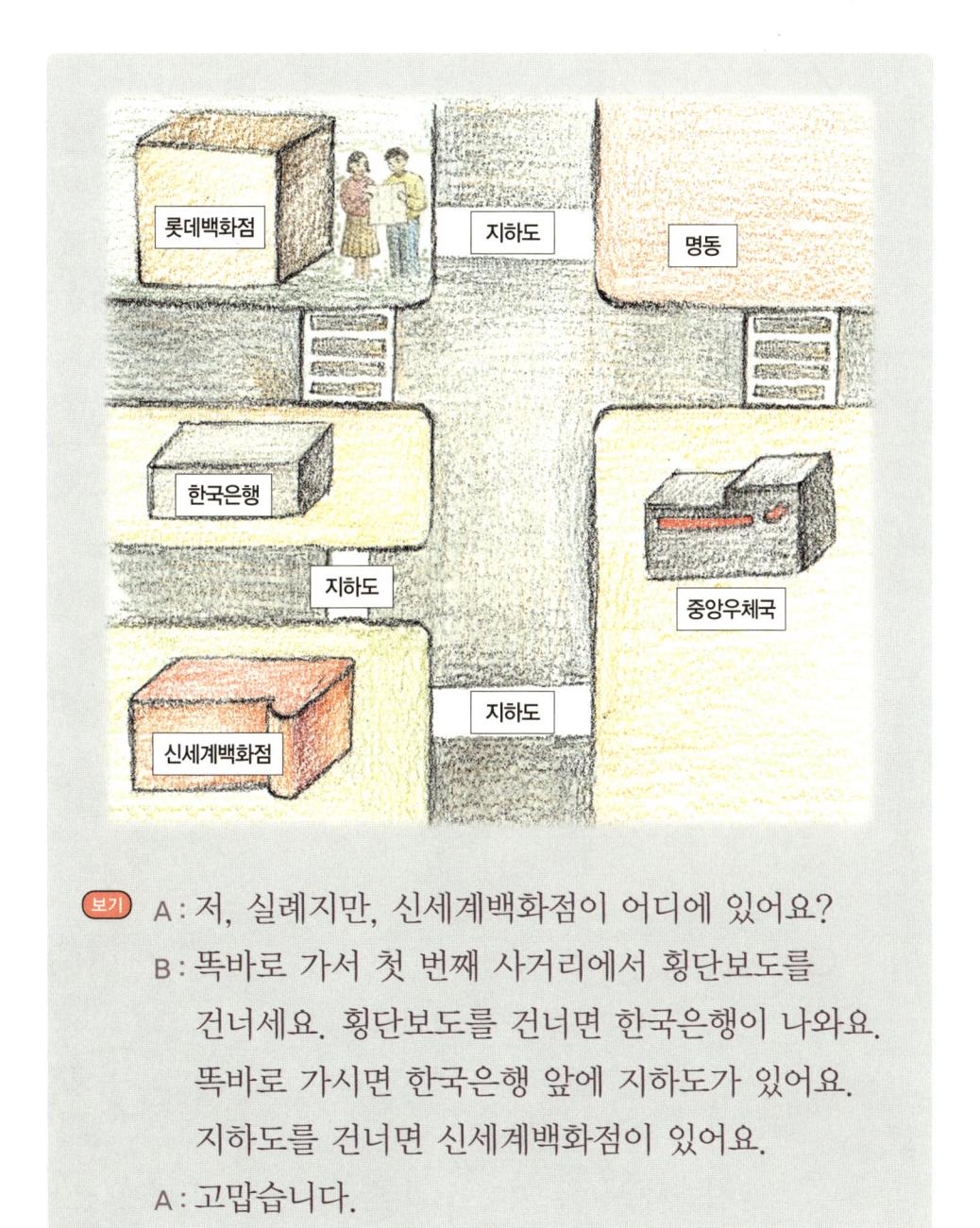

보기 A : 저, 실례지만, 신세계백화점이 어디에 있어요?
B : 똑바로 가서 첫 번째 사거리에서 횡단보도를 건너세요. 횡단보도를 건너면 한국은행이 나와요. 똑바로 가시면 한국은행 앞에 지하도가 있어요. 지하도를 건너면 신세계백화점이 있어요.
A : 고맙습니다.

097

>>> Talk 3

Explain how to get to your house by drawing your classmates a sketch map.

4

보기 우리 집은 신촌에 있어요.
근처에 현대백화점이 있어요.
현대백화점에서 지하도를 건너서 서강대학교 쪽으로 나가면 빵집이 있어요.
빵집에서 똑바로 2분쯤 가면 왼쪽에 우리 집이 있어요.

Finding your way 길 찾기

>>> Check Yourself

Evaluate your own improvement after studying this chapter.

	Poor	Fair	Good
I can ask for directions.			
I can give directions.			

우 회 전	좌 회 전	유 턴
주 차 금 지	자전거전용도로	보행자전용도로
택시승강장	버스정류장	지하철

Lesson 10 | Transportation 교통

••• Goals

- **Tasks:** Using transportation facilities and convenient facilities
- **Grammar:** -아/어/여야 되다
  -(으)로 갈아타다
- **Vocabulary & Expressions:** Transportation, train, subway stations and bus stops
- **Pronunciation:** /n/-insertion
- **Korean Culture:** Subway

>>> Get Ready

Have you ever taken a bus?
Which is faster, subway or bus?

Transportation 교통

••• Listen

Listen to the following conversation and repeat.

톰 스미스: 종합운동장에 가고 싶어요. 몇 번 버스를 타야 돼요?

박 미 선: 150번을 타세요. 시청역에서 내려서 지하철로 갈아타세요.

톰 스미스: 지하철 몇 호선을 타야 돼요?

박 미 선: 2호선을 타세요.

톰 스미스: 지금 시간에는 지하철이 복잡하겠지요?

박 미 선: 네, 그렇지만 지하철이 제일 빨라요.

여기 here	어떻게 how	가다 to go	타다 to take	내리다 to get off
갈아타다 to transfer	호선 line	복잡하다 to be crowded		제일 the most
빠르다 to be fast				

101

••• Vocabulary

Vocabulary plays an important role in speaking fluent Korean. Check out the following words.

택시	비행기	버스
버스 정류장	기차 역	공항
자전거	배	걷기

>>> Speak

••• Grammar

Grammar is also an important factor in speaking Korean fluently. Look at the following grammar points.

1. -아/어/여야 되다

We use this pattern to express obligation or necessity with a similar meaning to must, have to, should, or ought to in English. The basic form of '돼요' is '되다' and the following shows the correct forms.

> 예문 내일 시험이 있어서 열심히 공부해야 돼요.
> I have to study very hard because I have a test tomorrow.
>
> 일본에서 친구가 와서 오전에 공항에 가야 됩니다.
> I have to go to the airport in this morning because my friend is coming from Japan.
>
> 한국에서 일하고 싶으면 한국말을 배워야 돼요.
> You have to learn Korean if you want to work in Korea.

2. -(으)로 갈아타다

This expression is translated as 'transfer to' or 'change to' the other transportation.

> 예문 먼저 150번 버스를 타고 가십시오. First take the bus number 150.
>
> 그리고 시청 앞에서 지하철로 갈아타십시오.
> And then transfer to the subway at City Hall.
>
> 학교 앞에서 38번 버스를 타세요.
> Take the bus number 38 in front of the school.
>
> 그리고 시청 앞에서 103번 버스로 갈아타세요.
> And change to number 103 at City Hall.
>
> 지하철 1호선을 타십시오. Take subway line number one.
>
> 그리고 서울역에서 4호선으로 갈아타십시오.
> And change to line four at Seoul Station.

••• Practice

Look at the picture below and practice the conversation as suggested by the following example.

| 신촌 → 종로 3가 | 지하철 2호선, 을지로 3가역, 3호선 (20분) |

보기
A: 신촌에서 종로 3가까지 어떻게 가요?
B: 지하철 2호선을 타세요.
   을지로 3가역에서 3호선으로 갈아타세요.
A: 시간이 얼마나 걸릴까요?
B: 20분 쯤 걸려요.

①

| 광화문 → 코엑스 | 470번 버스, 강남역, 지하철 2호선 (30분) |

②

| 이화여대 → 대학로 | 지하철 2호선, 동대문 운동장역, 4호선 (25분) |

-번 number

••• Pronunciation

Listen and repeat.

1. 시청역
2. 색연필
3. 꽃잎
4. 나뭇잎

Transportation 교통

>>> Talk 1

Look at the route map below and discuss with your partner how to get to each destination below.

- 1) 신촌역 → 용산역
- 2) 불광역 → 시청역
- 3) 동대문운동장역 → 강남구청

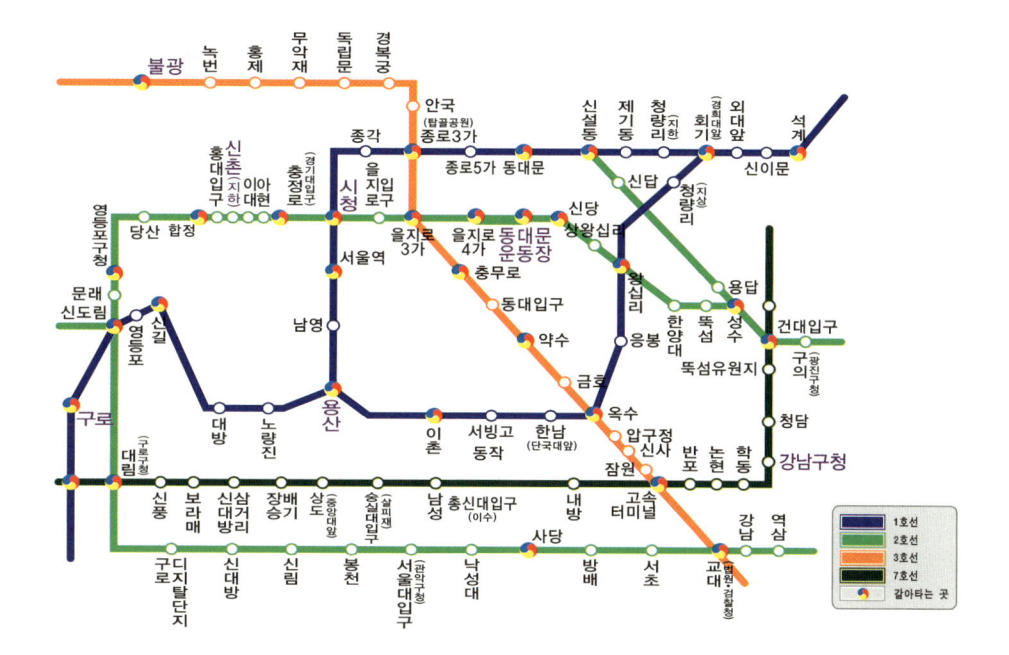

보기
A : 신촌역에서 용산역에 가고 싶어요.
어떻게 가야 돼요?
B : 시청역에서 내려서 1호선으로 갈아타세요.
서울역 방향 지하철을 타셔야 돼요.

방향 direction

105

>>> Talk 2

You are on the street. Choose one type of transportation from below and explain the reason as the following example suggests.

교통 수단 (transportation)	특 징 (characteristics)	시 간 (travel time)	요 금 (fare)
택 시	편안하다, 막힌다, 비싸다	25분	8,000원
버 스	싸다, 복잡하다, 막힌다	35분	900원
지하철	싸다, 빠르다, 복잡하다	20분	900원

보기 저는 택시를 타겠어요.
버스나 지하철에는 사람이 많아서 복잡해요.
그리고 앉아서 갈 수 없어요.
택시는 비싸지만 앉아서 갈 수 있어요.
그래서 택시를 타겠어요.

편안하다 to be comfortable   막히다 to have a traffic jam   싸다 to be cheap

>>> Korean Culture

The subway is one of the major transportations in Korea. It offers many services for a reasonable fare. Each subway station is conveniently connected to public buildings, places of historic interest, shopping malls and bus stations, etc. You can take a subway in big cities like Seoul, Incheon, Daegu and Busan. The subway services in Seoul is especially extensive. The opening of line 1 in 1974, the Seoul subway now serves the energetic city with 8 lines.

Transportation 교통

>>> Talk 3

Are there any places that you would recommend to visit in Korea? Choose a place and explain how to get there as the following example suggests.

> **보기** 산책을 좋아하면 덕수궁에 가세요.
> 덕수궁에는 나무와 꽃이 많이 있어서
> 산책하기 좋아요.
> 지하철 2호선을 타고 시청역에서 내리세요.
> 2번 출구 앞에 덕수궁이 있어요.

출구 exit

>>> Check Yourself

Evaluate your own improvement after studying this chapter.

	Poor	Fair	Good
I can ask and give street directions.			
I can use public transportation.			

Lesson 11 | Hobby
취미

••• Goals

- **Tasks:** Asking and answering questions about hobbies
- **Grammar:** −고
  −아/어/여 보다
- **Vocabulary & Expressions:** Vocabulary for hobbies
- **Pronunciation:** Palatalization
- **Korean Culture:** Online Community, Game Room

>>> Get Ready

Do you have any hobbies?
What do you usually do on Sundays?

Hobby 취미

••• Listen

Listen to the following conversation and repeat.

김미정 : 운동 좋아하세요?

이영수 : 네, 저는 스키를 좋아해요.

김미정 : 스키요?

이영수 : 네, 신나고 재미있어요.

김미정 : 그래요? 저도 타 보고 싶어요.

이영수 : 스키장에 같이 가요. 가르쳐 드릴게요.

신나다 to be exciting, enjoyable, delightful   한번 a time, once   같이 together

109

●●● Vocabulary

Vocabulary plays an important role in speaking fluent Korean. Check out the following words.

낚시 하기	영화 보기	사진 찍기
등산 하기	그림 그리기	책 읽기
야구	스키	축구

Hobby 취미

| 테니스 | 수영 | 농구 |

| >>> Korean Culture |

In Korea, people who share the same interests or hobbies gather together on line. This is called 'Internet society', which is getting increasingly popular as the use of Internet becomes widespread. The members of the Internet society exchange information on their hobbies, and have regular off-line meetings.

>>> Speak

••• Grammar

Grammar is also an important factor in speaking Korean fluently. Look at the following grammar points.

1. -고

'-고', attached to the verb and adjective stem, connects two sentences like the sentence linking conjunction 'and' in English.

> 예문 스키는 신나고 재미있어요. Skiing is exciting and fun.
> 한국 사람은 친절하고 부지런합니다. The Koreans are kind and diligent.
> 비가 오고 바람이 붑니다. It is raining and windy.

111

2. -아/어/여 보다

'-아/어/여 보다' usually takes the past tense form such as '-아/어/여 봤어요' or '-아/어/여 봤습니다'. In statements it expresses the experience, and in the imperative sentences it expresses advice or suggestion for the listener to try something.

예문 제주도에 가 봤어요? Have you ever been to Jeju Island?

한국 음식을 많이 먹어 봤어요. I have tried Korean food lots of times.

이 옷을 한번 입어 보십시오. Try this clothes on.

••• Practice

Look at the picture below and practice the conversation as suggested by the following example.

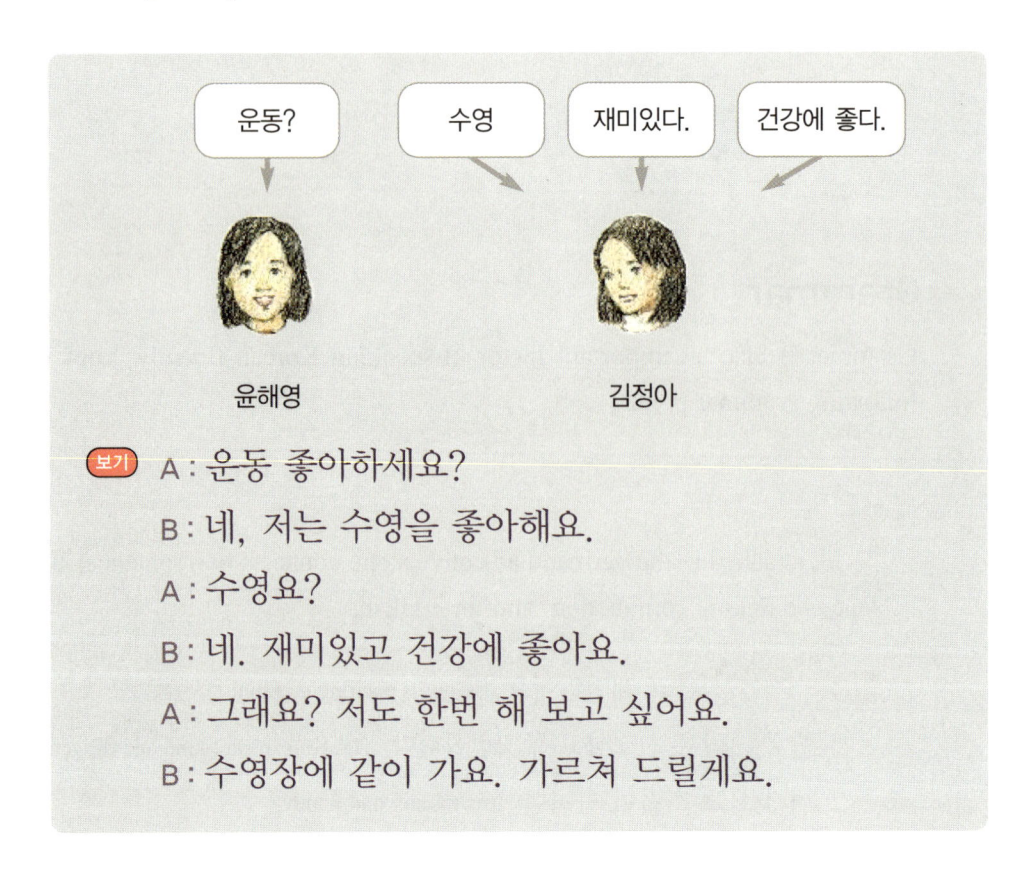

운동?   수영   재미있다.   건강에 좋다.

윤해영   김정아

보기 A : 운동 좋아하세요?
B : 네, 저는 수영을 좋아해요.
A : 수영요?
B : 네. 재미있고 건강에 좋아요.
A : 그래요? 저도 한번 해 보고 싶어요.
B : 수영장에 같이 가요. 가르쳐 드릴게요.

Hobby 취미

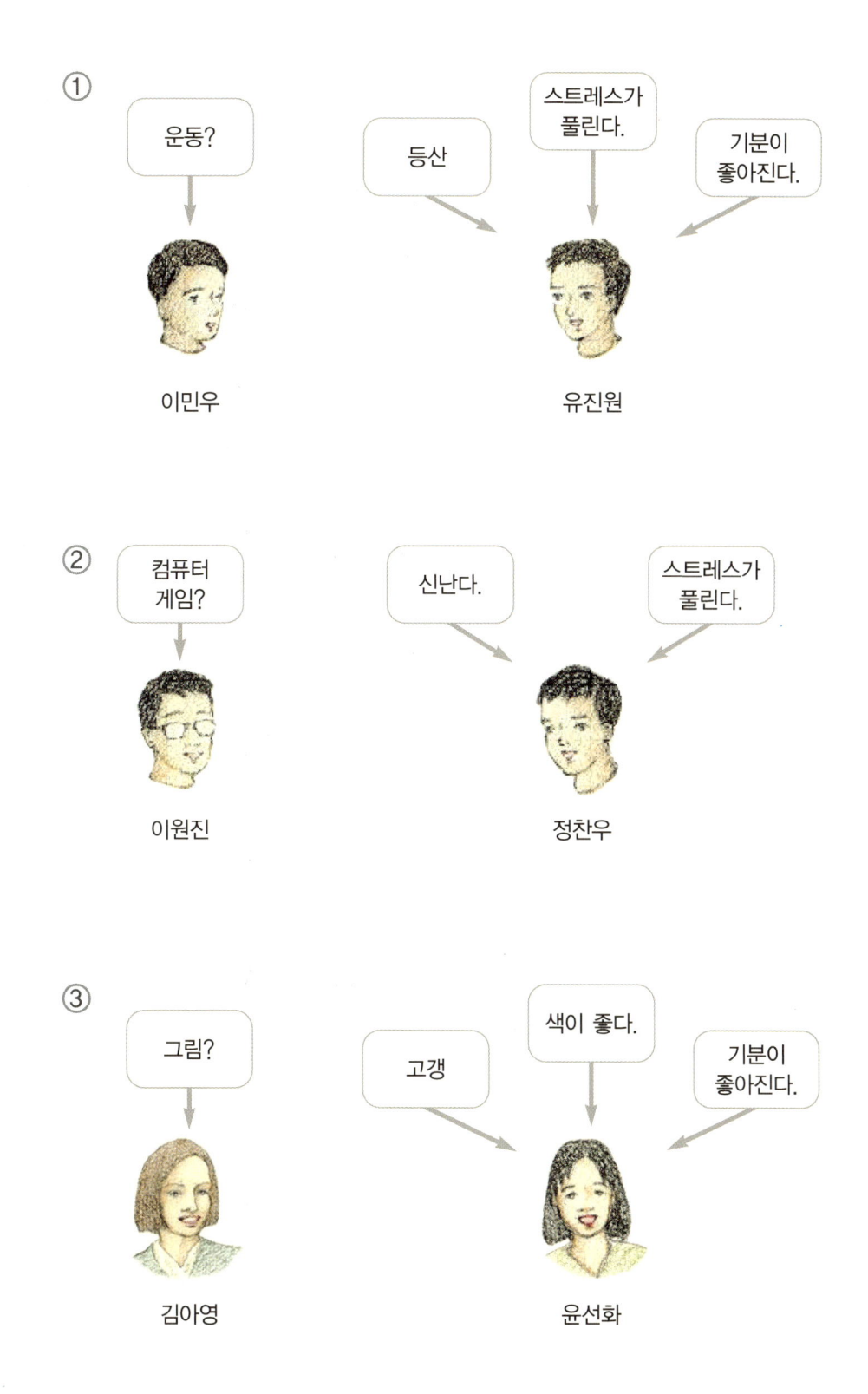

① 운동? → 이민우

등산 → 유진원 ← 스트레스가 풀린다. / 기분이 좋아진다.

② 컴퓨터 게임? → 이원진

신난다. → 정찬우 ← 스트레스가 풀린다.

③ 그림? → 김아영

고갱 → 윤선화 ← 색이 좋다. / 기분이 좋아진다.

113

건강에 좋다 to be good for health   스트레스가 풀리다 to get rid of stress
기분이 좋아지다 to feel better

>>> Korean Culture

There are many kinds of '방(rooms)' in Korea. 'PC방(Personal Computer Room)' along with 노래(singing)방 and 찜질(hot sauna)방, is very popular. PC방 charges an hourly rate, and many young (korean) people spend their free time enjoying online games ac PC방 equipped with the latest model PC with high-speed Internet access.

••• Pronunciation

Listen and repeat.

1. 같이
2. 해돋이
3. 끝이에요.

>>> Talk 1

The followings are the pictures of hobbies. Please choose one among them and guess what kind of hobby it is as the example shows.

스키 타기

인라인 스케이트 타기

Hobby 취미

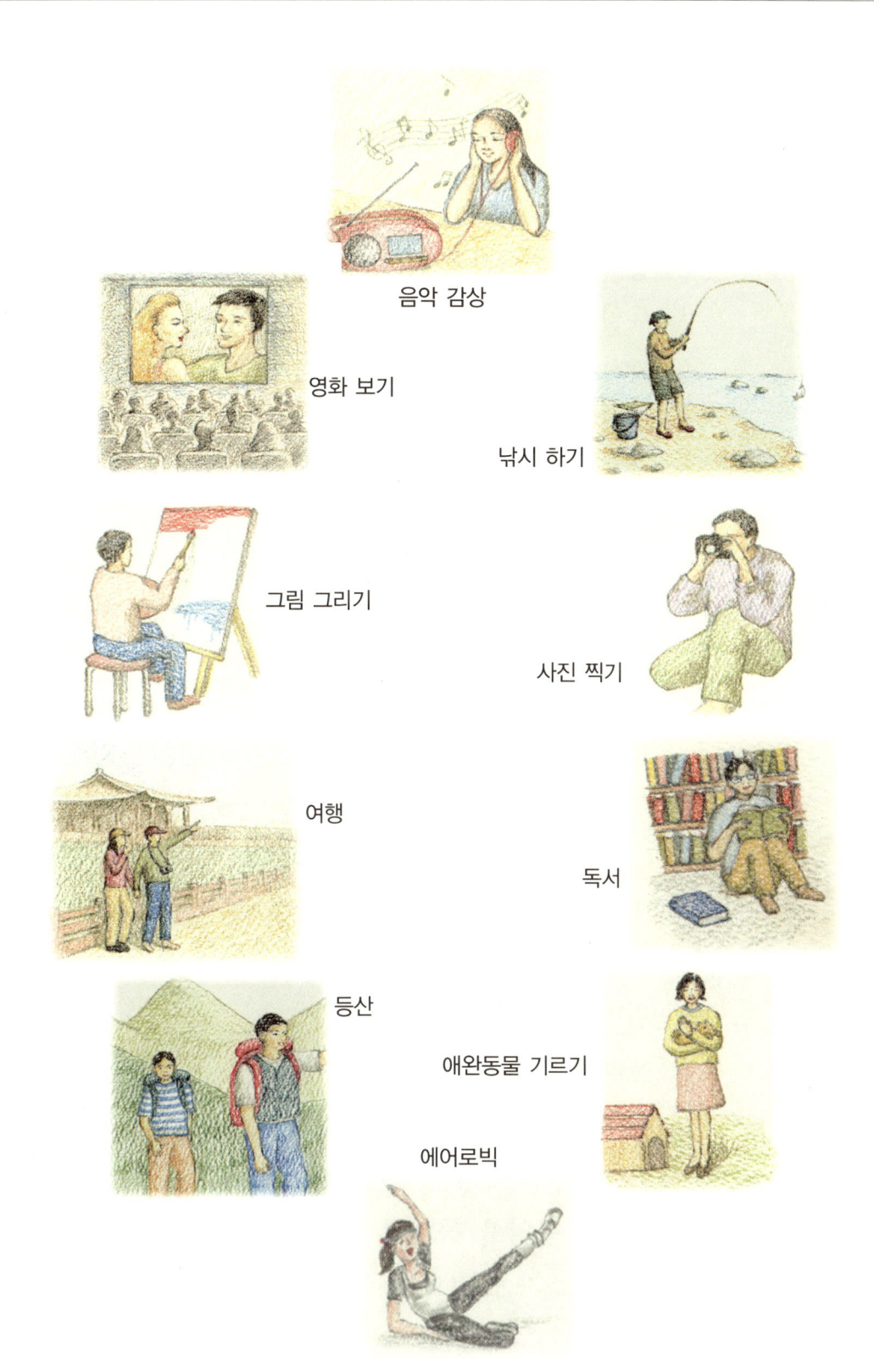

음악 감상

영화 보기

낚시 하기

그림 그리기

사진 찍기

여행

독서

등산

애완동물 기르기

에어로빅

> 보기 A : 언제 해요?
>
> B : 시간이 있을 때 해요.
>
> A : 어디에서 해요?
>
> B : 집 안하고 밖에서 다 할 수 있어요.
>
> A : 무엇이 필요해요?
>
> B : 사진기가 필요해요.
>
> A : 사진 찍기요.
>
> B : 맞아요.

필요하다 to need   사진기 camera   맞아요. That's right.

>>> Talk 2

Talk about your hobbies and discuss their advantages and disadvantages.

> 보기 A : 취미가 뭐예요?
>
> B : 음악 감상이에요.
>
> A : 음악 감상요?
>
> B : 네, 저는 클래식을 좋아해요.
>   클래식 음악을 들으면 기분이 좋아지고
>   스트레스가 풀려요.

>>> Talk 3

Talk about your hobbies to your classmates. If you do not have any hobbies, talk about the things that you usually do in your free time as the following example suggests.

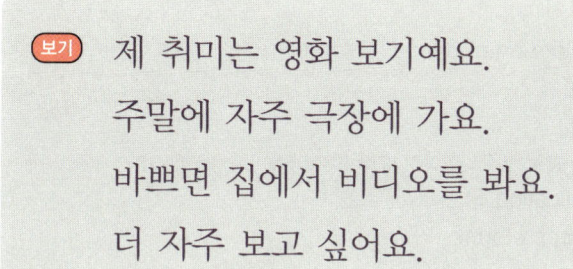

> 보기 제 취미는 영화 보기예요.
> 주말에 자주 극장에 가요.
> 바쁘면 집에서 비디오를 봐요.
> 더 자주 보고 싶어요.

자주 often

>>> Check Yourself

Evaluate your own improvement after studying this chapter.

	Poor	Fair	Good
I can ask and answer questions about hobbies.			
I can explain my hobbies.			

Lesson 12 | Items
물건

••• Goals
- **Tasks:** Describing colors and shapes, Describing selling and buying goods
- **Grammar:** –아/어/여 주세요
  -(으)ㄴ/는 1
- **Vocabulary & Expressions:** Colors and shapes
- **Pronunciation:** Tensification 2
- **Korean Culture:** Address terms

>>> Get Ready

What do you consider first when buying something?
When considering a purchase, what is the most important factor-price, style or quality?

118

Items 물건

••• Listen

Listen to the following conversation and repeat.

박미선 : 저, 아저씨, 가방 좀 보여 주세요.
점 원 : 어떤 걸 찾으세요?
박미선 : 여행 가방요. 편하고 가벼운 거 없어요?
점 원 : 이건 어떠세요? 요즘 잘 팔려요.
박미선 : 모양은 괜찮은데……. 다른 색은 없어요?
점 원 : 네, 그건 파란색밖에 없어요.

여행 travel	편하다 to be comfortable	가볍다 to be light	모양 shape
색깔 color	-밖에 only, nothing but		

119

| >>> Korean Culture |

The appellations to address one's relatives in the past are now used as general terms in modern Korean society. For example, '아주머니 (aunt)' or '아저씨 (uncle)' was only used when addressing one's aunt or uncle. But nowadays, they are used when addressing someone elder than oneself. Also '언니 (elder sister)' and '오빠 (elder brother)' are commonly spoken when calling shop assistants or strangers. But traditionally, these words were used when a girl called her elder sister or brother. Though this trend has become common place, the old generation thinks negatively of it.

••• Vocabulary

Vocabulary plays an important role in speaking fluent Korean. Check out the following words.

가방	우산	비누	빗	셔츠
바지	구두	지갑	운동화	치마
두껍다	얇다	부드럽다	딱딱하다	크다

Items 물건

| 작다 | 무겁다 | 가볍다 | 편하다 | 불편하다 |

하얀색 회색 밤색 빨간색 보라색

검은색 파란색 노란색 녹색

>>> **Speak**

••• Grammar

Grammar is also an important factor in speaking Korean fluently. Look at the following grammar points.

1. -아/어/여 주세요

We use this pattern when we require or ask something. If the beneficiary is the elder, '-아/어/여 드리세요' is used.

예문 가방 좀 보여 주세요. Show me some bags, please.

이것 좀 들어 주세요. Hold this, please.

내일 오후에 전화해 주세요. Call me tomorrow afternoon, please.

121

2. -(으)ㄴ/는 1

'-(으)ㄴ/는' is attached to the adjective stem to modify the noun following it. This noun modifier is in the present tense. '-는' is used after the adjectives ending with '있다/없다', and '-(으)ㄴ' is used after all the other adjectives.

예문 예쁜 모자가 있어요. There is a pretty hat.

좋은 영화를 봤어요. I watched a good movie.

재미있는 책을 읽어요. I am reading an interesting book.

••• Practice

Look at the picture below and practice the conversation as suggested by the following example.

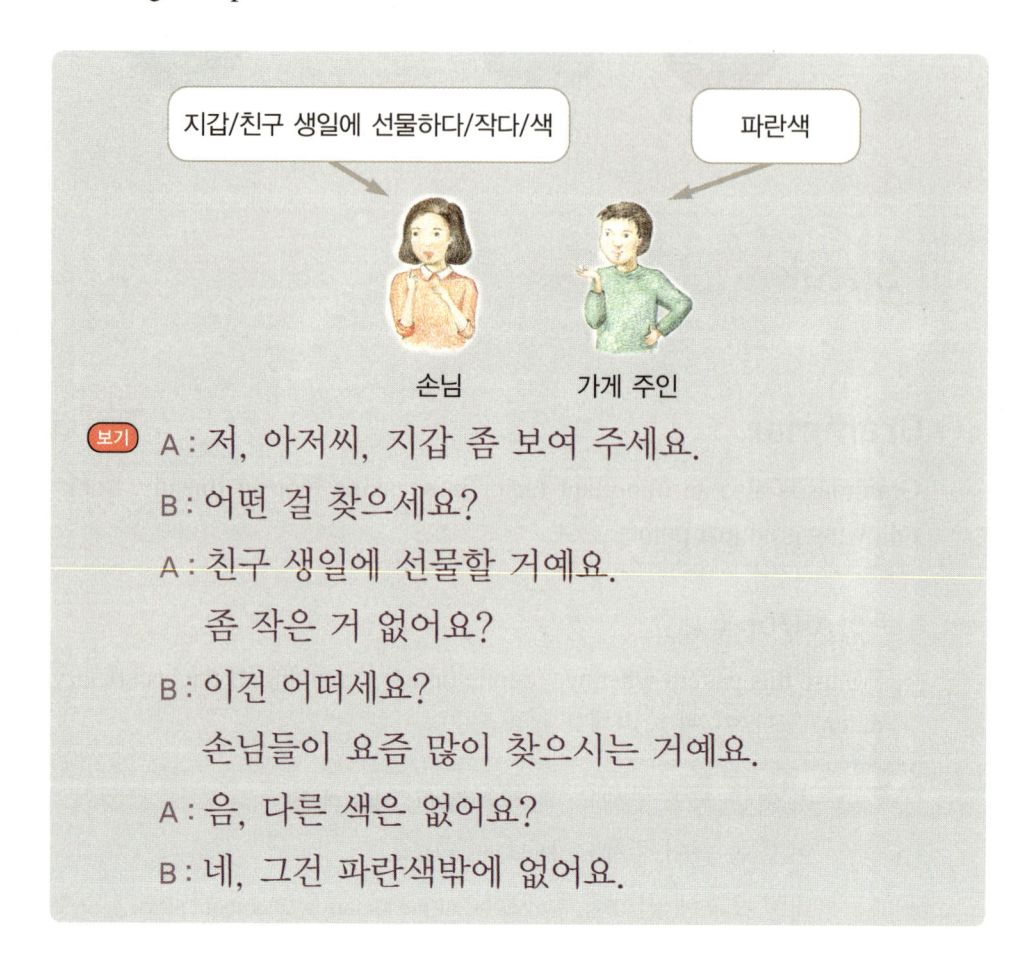

지갑/친구 생일에 선물하다/작다/색

파란색

손님

가게 주인

보기 A : 저, 아저씨, 지갑 좀 보여 주세요.

B : 어떤 걸 찾으세요?

A : 친구 생일에 선물할 거예요.

좀 작은 거 없어요?

B : 이건 어떠세요?

손님들이 요즘 많이 찾으시는 거예요.

A : 음, 다른 색은 없어요?

B : 네, 그건 파란색밖에 없어요.

Items 물건

① 손님: 우산/선물하다/가볍다/색
  가게 주인: 노란색

② 손님: 티셔츠/운동할 때 입다/편하다/큰 것
  가게 주인: 작은 것

③ 손님: 운동화/등산할 때 신다/가볍고 편하다/작은 것
  가게 주인: 큰 것

••• Pronunciation

Listen and repeat.

1. 쓸 건데요.
2. 갈 수 있어요.
3. 갈 데가 있어요.

123

>>> Talk 1

Choose one of the items from below and describe it as the following example suggests. Let others listen to you and guess what it is.

보기
A : 이것은 머리에 쓰는 거예요.
여러 가지 색과 모양이 있어요.
여름에 많이 써요.
이것을 쓰면 얼굴이 안 타요.
B : 모자예요.

Items 물건

>>> Talk 2

Choose a trip from the pictures below and discuss the items to bring for the trip as the following example suggests.

①

일주일 동안 바닷가에 여행을 가요.

②

2박 3일 동안 설악산 근처에 있는 이모 댁에 가요.

③

한 달 동안 중국 여행을 가요.

살 것들(things to buy)

50,000원
55,000원
80,000원
40,000원
42,000원
180,000원
8,500원
48,000원
62,000원
35,000원
53,000원
23,000원
85,000원
37,000원
10,000원
12,000원
9,000원

> [보기] A : 무엇을 살까요?
> B : 파라솔을 삽시다.
> A : 파라솔은 42,000원이에요. 비싸요.
> B : 그래도 필요하니까 삽시다.
> 　　그리고 선글라스도 사야 해요.
> A : 네, 좋아요. 슬리퍼도 필요하죠?
> B : 그래요.

Items 물건

>>> **Talk 3**

You want to sell some of the stuff you have used. Write down the items you wish to sell and describe them.

팔 물건	설명

>>> **Check Yourself**

Evaluate your own improvement after studying this chapter.

	Poor	Fair	Good
I can describe the colors and shapes of objects.			
I can describe objects.			
I can buy and sell goods.			

Lesson 13 | Telephone 전화

●●● Goals

- **Tasks:** Calling someone, Asking for someone
- **Grammar:** -한테서
  -(으)ㄴ/는데요
- **Vocabulary & Expressions:** Telephone, Reservation
- **Pronunciation:** Coda rule 2 - complex coda
- **Korean Culture:** Mobile phone

>>> Get Ready

Where is this person calling?

Have you ever made a reservation over the phone?

Telephone 전화

••• Listen

Listen to the following conversation and repeat.

조 영 민 : 여보세요. 미정이네 집이죠?

미정이 동생 : 네, 그런데요.

조 영 민 : 전 미정이 친구 영민인데요.
　　　　　　미정이 집에 있어요?

미정이 동생 : 지금 없는데요.

조 영 민 : 그럼, 영민이한테서 전화 왔다고 전해 주세요.

미정이 동생 : 네, 알겠습니다.

전하다 to give (a message)

••• Vocabulary

Vocabulary plays an important role in speaking fluent Korean. Check out the following words.

전화번호	telephone number	부재중	be absent
전화하다	to call	용건	message
전화를 받다	to answer the telephone	문의하다	to inquire
전화를 끊다	to hang up	예약	reservation
통화 중	The line is busy.	예약하다	to make a reservation

In what situation would you use these expressions?

상황	대화 내용
전화를 걸고 받을 때	가 : **여보세요**, 거기 서울식당입니까? 나 : 네, 그렇습니다. 가 : 여보세요, **김미정 씨 계십니까**? 나 : **전데요**. 누구십니까? 가 : 안녕하세요? 이영수입니다.
전화가 잘못 왔을 때	가 : 여보세요, 김미정씨 계십니까? 나 : **실례지만, 몇 번에 거셨습니까**? 가 : 거기 2123-4576이지요? 나 : 아닙니다. **잘못 거셨습니다**. 가 : 죄송합니다.
전화를 바꿀 때	가 : 한국대학교입니다. 누굴 찾으십니까? 나 : **김미정 씨 좀 바꿔 주세요**. 가 : 네, 잠깐만 기다리세요. 　(잠시 후) 다 : **전화 바꿨습니다**.

Telephone 전화

| >>> Korean Culture |

The mobile phone, first introduced to public in 1990, has become a must in modern Korean society since then. And nowadays, about 60% of Korean population have their own mobile phone. In addition to its function as a telephone, it can be used as a credit card or for phone banking. Lately, a new technology was introduced in Korea that allows the users to watch movies or listen to music, use Internet and take pictures all on the same mobile phone.

>>> Speak

••• Grammar

Grammar is also an important factor in speaking Korean fluently. Look at the following grammar points.

1. -한테서

Attached to a noun indicating a person or people, '-한테서' indicates the initiator of an action similar to 'from' in English.

> 예문 친구한테서 편지가 왔어요. I got a letter from my friend.
> 나는 부모님한테서 용돈을 받습니다. I get allowances from my parents.
> 영민이한테서 이 책을 빌렸습니다. I borrowed this book from Youngmin.

2. -(으)ㄴ/는데요

'-(으)ㄴ/는데요' has the effect of making the sentence sound a little softer than '-어요' or '-습니다' when explaining the situation. '-은데요' is attached to the adjective stem ending in a consonant, and 'ㄴ데요' is attached to the adjective stem ending in a vowel. '-는데요' is attached to the verb stem, '있다/없다', and the verb and adjective of past tense with '-았/었/였-'.

예문 A : 민수 씨 계십니까? Is Minsu in?
B : 지금 안 계신데요. No, he is not.

A : 맛이 어때요? How does it taste?
B : 맛이 정말 좋은데요. It tastes very good.

A : 제가 만든 음식 어때요? How do you like my dish?
B : 참 맛있는데요. It is very delicious.

••• Practice

Look at the picture below and practice the conversation as suggested by the following example.

경수에게

오경미   경수 누나

보기 A : 여보세요. 경수네 집이죠?
B : 네, 그런데요.
A : 전 경수 친구 경민데요. 경수 집에 있어요?
B : 지금 없는데요.
A : 그럼, 경미한테서 전화 왔다고 좀 전해 주세요?
B : 네, 알겠습니다.

Telephone 전화

①

민철이에게

황수진   민철이 아버지

②

현석이에게

문경미   현석이 어머니

③

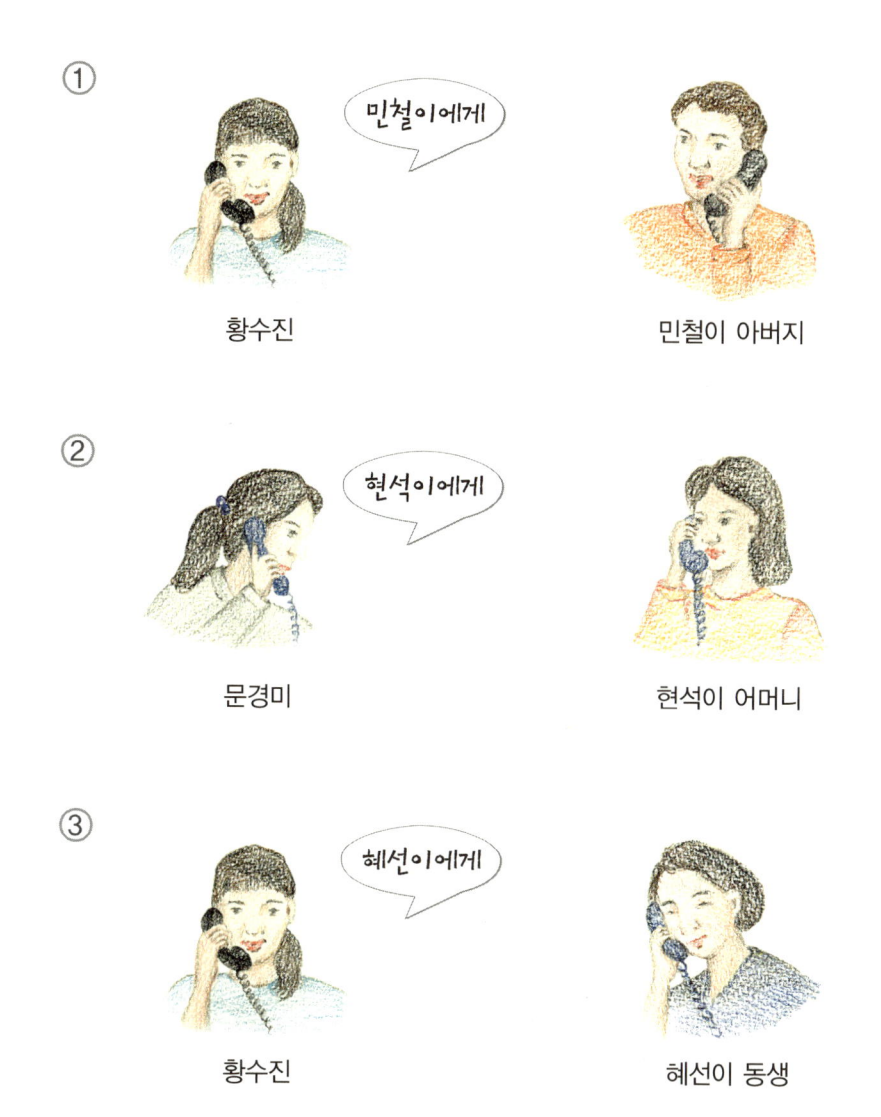

혜선이에게

황수진   혜선이 동생

••• Pronunciation

Listen and repeat.

1. 없는데요.
2. 앉다
3. 닮다

133

>>> Talk 1

You want to call a restaurant to make a reservation. Practice the phone conversation as the following example suggests.

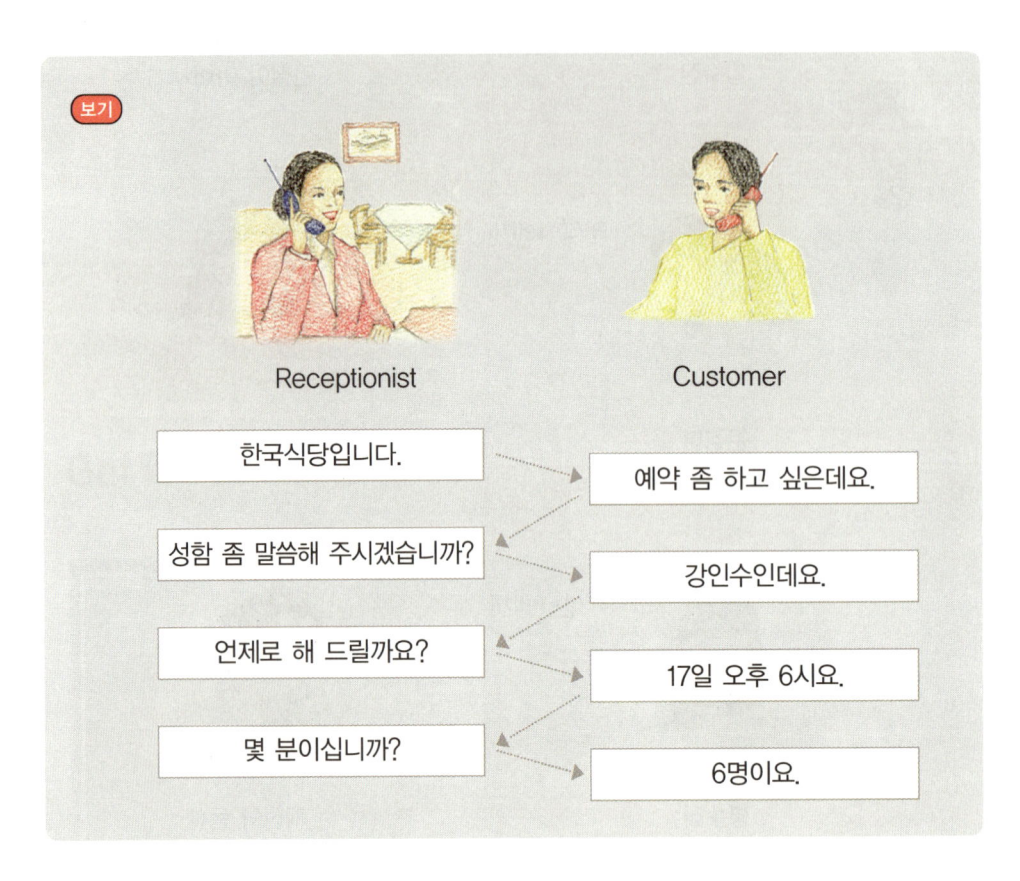

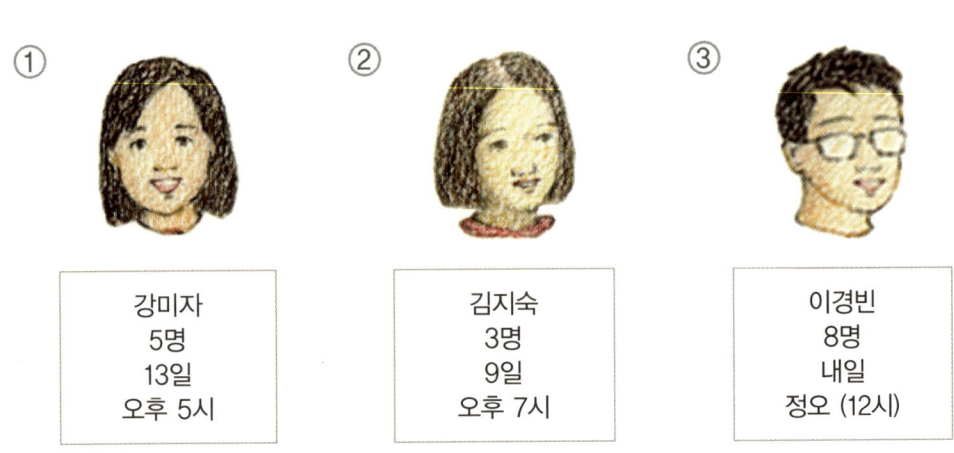

보기

Receptionist / Customer

- 한국식당입니다.
- 예약 좀 하고 싶은데요.
- 성함 좀 말씀해 주시겠습니까?
- 강인수인데요.
- 언제로 해 드릴까요?
- 17일 오후 6시요.
- 몇 분이십니까?
- 6명이요.

① 강미자
5명
13일
오후 5시

② 김지숙
3명
9일
오후 7시

③ 이경빈
8명
내일
정오 (12시)

Telephone 전화

>>> Talk 2

In Korea, when people want to know a phone number of some places or people, they call 114. Call 114 and inquire the numbers you would like to know.

> **보기**
> A : 네, 고객님.
> B : 한국대학교 전화번호 좀 가르쳐 주세요.
> A : 한국대학교 말씀이십니까?
> B : 네, 한국대학교요.
> A : 문의하신 번호는 지역 번호
>   02-359-2114번입니다.
>   359-2114번입니다.

문의하신 번호 the number you asked for

서울 역 : 392-7788
예술의 전당 : 580-1114
세종문화회관 : 399-1700
택시 호출 : 1588-0082

전화 번호는 다음과 같이 두 가지
방법으로 읽을 수 있어요.
359-2114 (삼오구에 이일일사)
(삼백오십구국에 이천백십사번)
다음 전화 번호를 한 번 읽어 보세요.
478-5423, 965-0945, 232-0016

>>> Talk 3

You called your friend, and heard the following message from the answering machine.

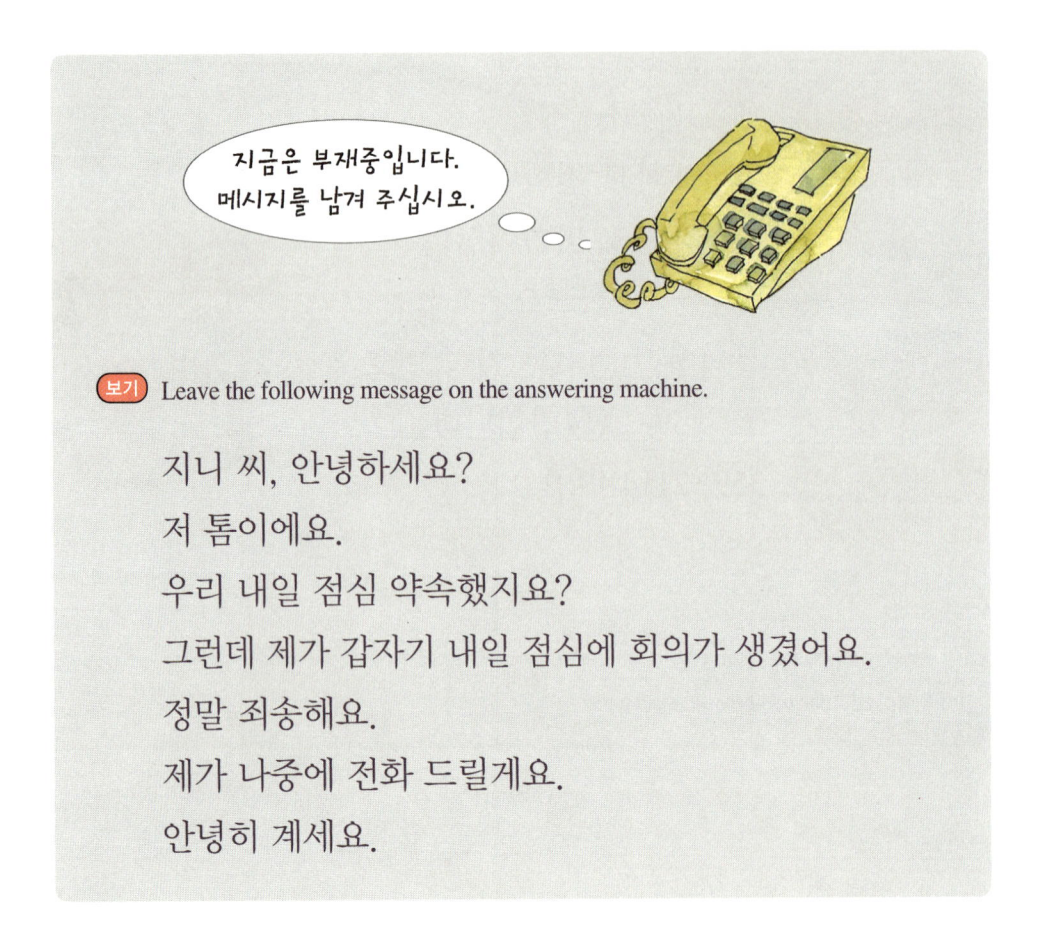

지금은 부재중입니다.
메시지를 남겨 주십시오.

보기) Leave the following message on the answering machine.

지니 씨, 안녕하세요?
저 톰이에요.
우리 내일 점심 약속했지요?
그런데 제가 갑자기 내일 점심에 회의가 생겼어요.
정말 죄송해요.
제가 나중에 전화 드릴게요.
안녕히 계세요.

| 갑자기 suddenly | 회의 meeting | 메시지 message | 죄송합니다. I'm sorry. |
| 생기다 to come up | | | |

Telephone 전화

>>> Check Yourself

Evaluate your own improvement after studying this chapter.

	Poor	Fair	Good
I can leave a message on the answering machine.			
I can use appropriate expressions when I make a phone call.			

Lesson 14 | Mail
우편

••• Goals
- **Tasks:** Using postal services
- **Grammar:** –(으)ㄹ 거예요
  –(이)나
- **Vocabulary & Expressions:** Post office-related vocabulary
- **Pronunciation:** Tensification 3
- **Korean Culture:** Express Delivery Service

>>> Get Ready

What do you go to the post office for?
Have you ever sent a letter or a small parcel?

Mail 우편

••• Listen

Listen to the following conversation and repeat.

이 영 수 : 이거 부산에 보내려고 하는데요.

우체국 직원 : 안에 뭐가 들었어요?

이 영 수 : 옷인데요.

우체국 직원 : 빠른우편으로 보내실 거예요?
보통우편으로 보내실 거예요?

이 영 수 : 보통우편으로요. 며칠이나 걸려요?

우체국 직원 : 삼사일 정도 걸립니다.

보통우편 regular mail   빠른우편 express mail   옷 clothes

| >>> Korean Culture |

'Quick service' is a quick parcel delivery service. While ordinary postal service takes more than two days to deliver a parcel, 'quick service' delivers a parcel to the destination within an hour. If a customer calls the nearest office, a motorbike delivery person comes to his/her doorstep to pick up the parcel. 'Quick service' is literally the quickest way to send things.

••• Vocabulary

Vocabulary plays an important role in speaking fluent Korean. Check out the following words.

편지	소포	우편물	내용물	봉투
서류 봉투	우표	우체통	보내다	포장하다/싸다

>>> Speak

••• Grammar

Grammar is also an important factor in speaking Korean fluently. Look at the following grammar points.

1. -(으)ㄹ 거예요

'-(으)ㄹ 거예요' expresses the speaker's intention or will. In questions, it is used to ask the intention of the listener. '-을 거예요' is attached to the verb or adjective stem ending in a consonant, and '-ㄹ 거예요' is attached to the verb or adjective stem ending in a vowel.

> 예문 내일 친구를 만날 거예요. I am going to meet my friend tomorrow.
>
> 빠른우편으로 보낼 거예요? Are you going to send this by express mail?
>
> 지금 저녁 먹을 거예요? Are you going to have dinner now?

2. -(이)나

Attached to numerical expressions, '-(이)나' indicates the estimate of numbers similar to 'approximately', 'roughly', 'about' etc. in English. '쯤' has the similar meaning.

> 예문 몇 개나 샀어요? Approximately, how many did you buy?
>
> 책이 몇 권이나 있어요? Roughly, how many books are there?
>
> 손님이 몇 분이나 오세요? Roughly, how many guests are you expecting?

••• Practice

Look at the picture below and practice the conversation as suggested by the following example.

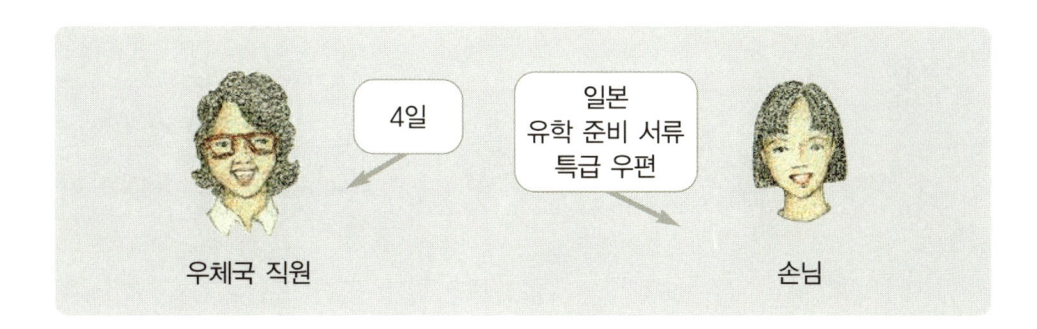

4일

일본
유학 준비 서류
특급 우편

우체국 직원   손님

[보기] 손님: 이거 일본에 보내려고 하는데요.
직원: 안에 뭐가 들었어요?
손님: 유학 준비 서류인데요.
직원: 특급 우편으로 보내실 거예요? 보통우편으로 보내실 거예요?
손님: 특급 우편으로요. 며칠이나 걸려요?
직원: 4일 정도 걸립니다.

① 손님 — 미국 / 책 / 보통우편 — 15일 — 우체국 직원

② 손님 — 전주 / 인삼 / 특급 우편 — 8시간 — 우체국 직원

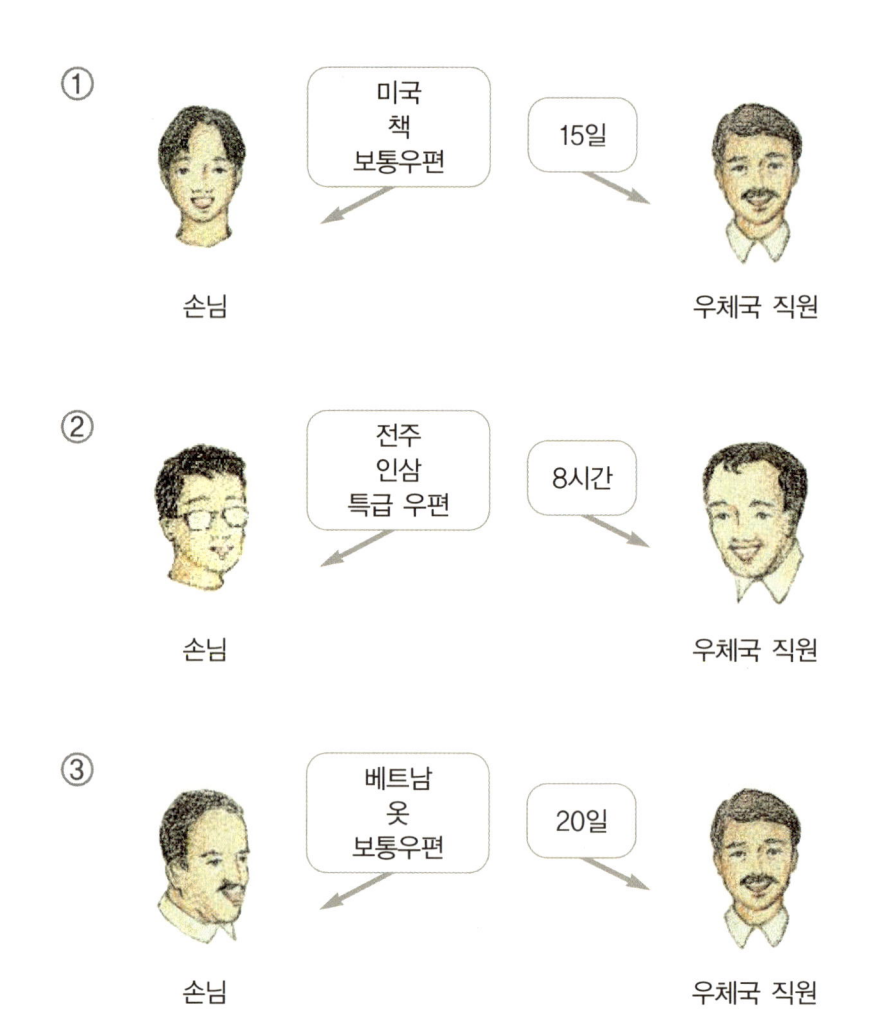

③ 손님 — 베트남 / 옷 / 보통우편 — 20일 — 우체국 직원

Mail 우편

유학 준비 서류 documents for preparing for study abroad   특급 우편 special delivery mail

••• Pronunciation

Listen and repeat.

1. 발달
2. 실수
3. 글자

>>> Talk 1

Rearrange the pictures in the correct order and tell the story.

요금 지불하기 (paying for postage)	번호표 뽑기 (taking a ticket)	기다리기 (waiting)
직원에게 물어보기 (asking a clerk)	우편 종류 선택하기 (selecting a postage type)	포장하기 (wrapping a package)

143

>>> Talk 2

The followings are the types of Korean postal services. Choose an item from below and decide which service you will use to send it. Practice the conversation as the following example suggests.

우편 종류	요금	도착 시간
보통우편	1,500원	4일 이내
빠른우편	2,500원	보낸 다음 날
특급 우편	4,000원	약 10시간 이내

인삼 1kg

핸드백 한 개

사과 한 상자

책 두 권

서류

꽃 바구니

보기
A : 내용물이 뭐예요?
B : 인삼이에요.
A : 어떻게 보내실 거예요?
B : 보통우편으로 보낼 거예요. 얼마나 걸릴까요?
A : 4일 정도 걸립니다.

Mail 우편

| 우편 종류 postal type | 요금 (postal) rate | 도착 시간 arrival time |

>>> Talk 3

What are the kinds of postal services available in your country? Introduce the postal system in your country by comparing it to the Korean one.

한국의 우체국	여러분 나라의 우체국
· 편지를 보내요 · 소포를 보내요 · 돈을 예금해요 · 돈을 송금해요 · 여러 가지 물건을 사요	

| 예금하다 to deposit | 송금하다 to wire money online |

>>> Check Yourself

Evaluate your own improvement after studying this chapter.

	Poor	Fair	Good
I can send letters and packages at the post office.			
I can understand how to use the services available at the post office.			

145

Lesson 15 | Appearance
외모

••• Goals
- **Tasks:** Describing appearance and clothing
- **Grammar:** -고 있다
  -(으)ㄴ 2, -는 2
- **Vocabulary & Expressions:** Appearance and clothing-related vocabulary
- **Pronunciation:** Comparison of plain stops, fortes stops and aspirated stops
- **Korean Culture:** Pointing a person, Surname (last name)

>>> Get Ready

How do you find someone in a crowded place?
What are some of the features you can use to decribe a person?

Appearance 외모

••• Listen

Listen to the following conversation and repeat.

김미정 : 정훈 씨가 누구예요?

박미선 : 저기 계신 분이에요.

김미정 : 어느 분요?

박미선 : 키가 크고 파란 양복을 입고 있는 분이에요.

김미정 : 저 쪽에 둥근 안경을 끼고 계신 분요?

| >>> Korean Culture |

In Korea, it is considered impolite to point at someone with one's finger. You can point someone who is far from you to indicate the exact location. However, when you wish to specify someone next to you or you are talking to, you have to hold your palm upward and point your entire palm towards the person.

••• Vocabulary

Vocabulary plays an important role in speaking fluent Korean. Check out the following words.

양복	구두	배낭	넥타이
모자	안경	쓰다	입다
매다	쓰다	날씬하다	뚱뚱하다

>>> Speak

••• Grammar

Grammar is also an important factor in speaking Korean fluently. Look at the following grammar points.

1. -고 있다

Usually '-고 있다' indicates an action in progress. However, as used in this lesson, it also can indicate the lasting result of an action when used with such verbs as '입다', '신다', '쓰다', '끼다', and '들다'.

> **예문** 수민 씨가 청바지를 입고 있어요. Sumin is wearing blue jeans
>
> 민호 씨가 둥근 안경을 끼고 있어요.
> Minho is wearing round shaped glasses.
>
> 그 사람은 노란 모자를 쓰고 있어요. S/he is wearing a yellow hat.

2. -(으)ㄴ 2, -는 2

Attached to the verb stem, '-(으)ㄴ' or '-는' modifies the noun following it. '-는' is the present form and '-(으)ㄴ' is the past form of this modifier.

> **예문** 내가 사는 동네는 조용합니다. The town I live in is a quiet place.
>
> 우리 어머니가 만드시는 요리는 참 맛있습니다.
> The dishes my mother makes are very delicious.
>
> 어제 그 영화 본 사람 있어요? Is there anyone who saw seen that movie yesterday?
>
> 이 책이 어제 산 책입니다. This is the book I bought yesterday.

••• Practice

Look at the picture below and practice the conversation as suggested by the following example.

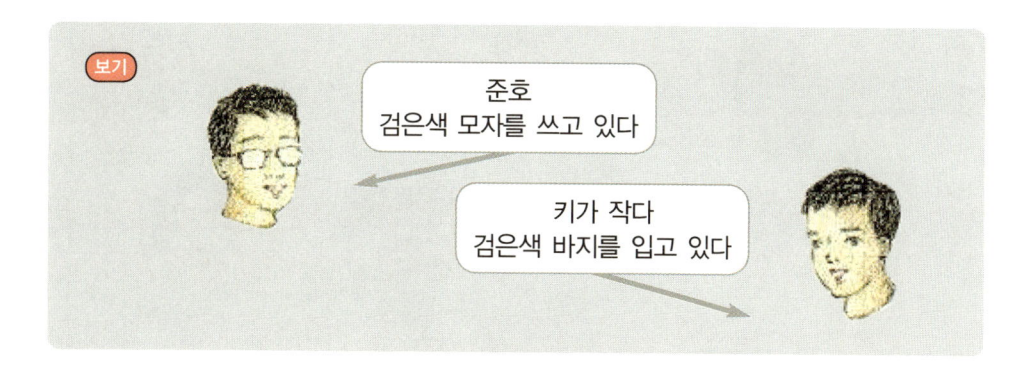

보기

준호
검은색 모자를 쓰고 있다

키가 작다
검은색 바지를 입고 있다

보기
A: 준호 씨가 누구예요?
B: 저기 계신 분이에요.
A: 어느 분요?
B: 키가 작고 검은색 바지를 입고 있는 분이에요.
A: 아, 저쪽에 검은색 모자를 쓰고 계신 분요?

① 제니
배낭을 메고 있다

얼굴이 둥글다
긴 치마를 입고 있다

②  민호
큰 가방을 들고 있다

뚱뚱하다
노란 넥타이를 매고 있다

③  미정
모자를 쓰고 있다

청바지에 운동화를
신고 있다

Appearance 외모

••• Pronunciation

Listen and repeat.

1. 굴, 꿀
2. 공, 콩
3. 달, 탈, 딸
4. 사다, 싸다
5. 자다, 차다, 짜다
6. 바다, 파다

>>> Talk 1

Work with a partner. Describe one of the pictures below, while your partner is asked to guess who you are referring to as the following example suggests.

① 영진　② 미영　③ 수진　④ 경수

> 보기　A: 모자를 쓴 사람이에요.
> 　　　작은 가방을 들고 있는 사람이에요.
> 　　　누구일까요?
> 　　　B: 미영 씨요.

151

>>> Talk 2

Under each situation described below, advise your friend on what to wear. Practice the conversation as the following example suggests.

상황	복장
친구가 회사에 면접을 보러 가려고 합니다.	단정한 옷 – 넥타이, 양복
친구가 음악회에 가려고 합니다.	
친구가 데이트를 하러 가려고 합니다.	
친구가 등산을 가려고 합니다.	

보기
A: 어떤 옷을 입으면 좋을까요?
B: 면접을 보러 가죠?
   그러면 단정한 옷을 입으세요.
A: 단정한 옷요?
B: 네, 넥타이를 매고 양복을 입으세요.

단정하다 to be neat

>>> Talk 3

Ask your friend to pick up your parents from the airport. Describe their appearances to him/her based on the pictures below.

Appearance 외모

① ② ③

보기 우리 아버지는 키가 크고 안경을 끼셨어요.
그리고, 빨간색 큰 가방을 들고 계세요.
우리 어머니는 키가 작고 노란색 모자를 쓰고 계세요.

>>> Check Yourself

Evaluate your own improvement after studying this chapter.

	Poor	Fair	Good
I can describe a person's appearance.			
I can describe a person's clothing.			

Lesson 16 | Bank 은행

●●● Goals

- **Tasks:** Depositing, withdrawing and exchanging money at the bank
- **Grammar:** −아/어/여야 하다
  −(으)려고 하다
- **Vocabulary & Expressions:** Vocabulary necessary at the bank
- **Pronunciation:** Liaison 2
- **Korean Culture:** ID cards, Foreign exchange

>>> Get Ready

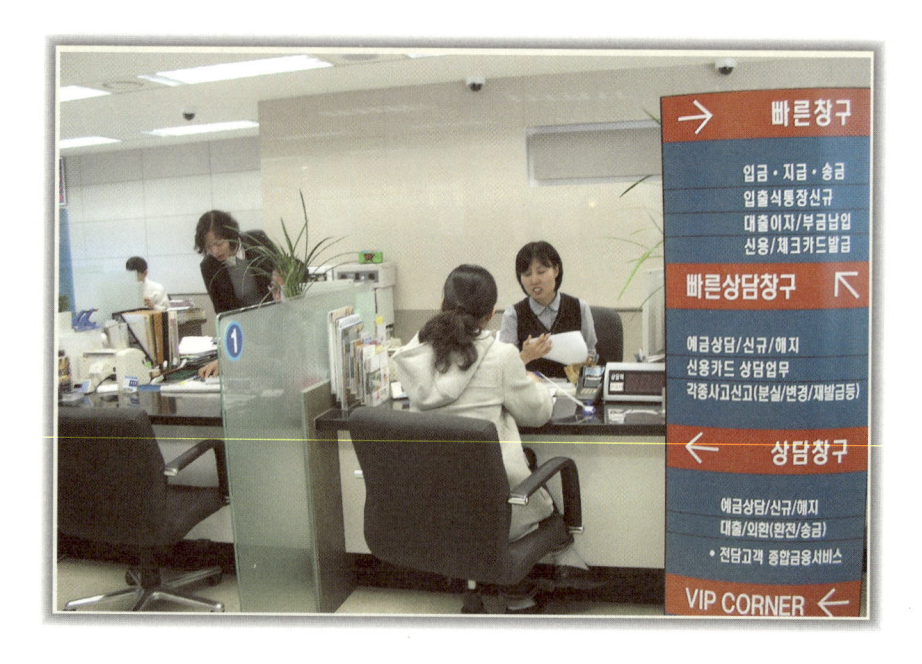

Do you go to the bank often?

What are the services available at the bank?

Bank 은행

••• Listen

Listen to the following conversation and repeat.

은행원 : 어서 오세요.

김미정 : 돈을 보내려고 하는데요.

은행원 : 통장하고 도장을 주시겠어요?

김미정 : 여기 있어요.

은행원 : 여기에 은행 이름과 계좌 번호를 써 주세요. 수수료는 1,000원입니다.

김미정 : 네, 여기요.

은행 bank   수수료 service charge, fee

••• Vocabulary

Vocabulary plays an important role in speaking fluent Korean. Check out the following words.

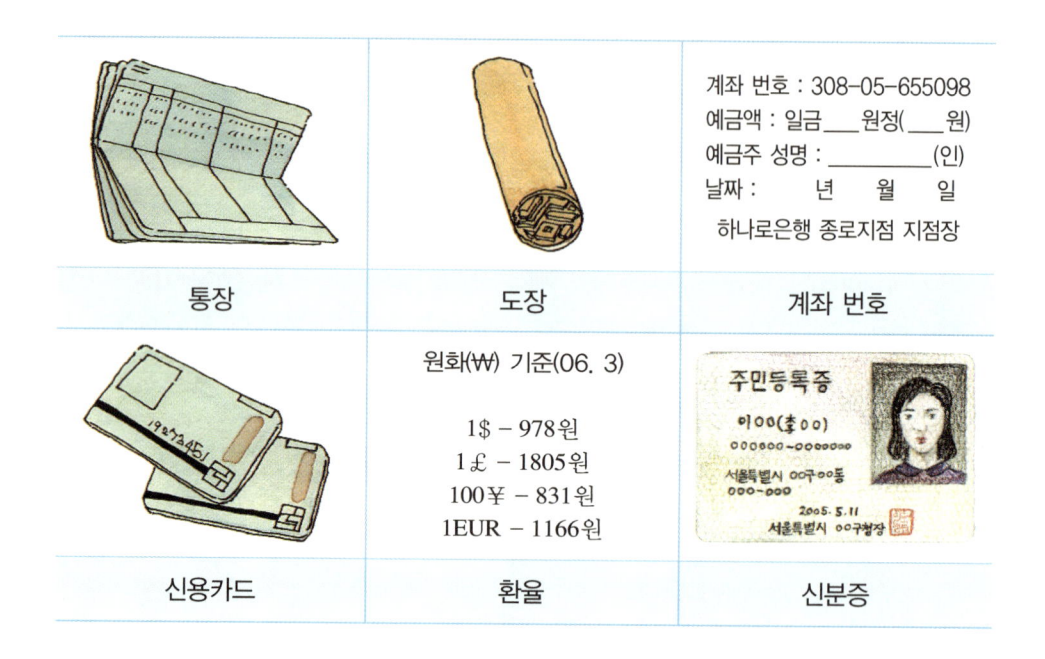

통장	도장	계좌 번호
신용카드	환율	신분증

원화(₩) 기준(06. 3)

1$ − 978원
1£ − 1805원
100¥ − 831원
1EUR − 1166원

계좌 번호 : 308-05-655098
예금액 : 일금___원정(___원)
예금주 성명 : _____(인)
날짜 :   년   월   일
하나로은행 종로지점 지점장

>>> Speak

••• Grammar

Grammar is also an important factor in speaking Korean fluently. Look at the following grammar points.

1. -아/어/여야 하다

We use this pattern to express obligation or necessity(with a similar meaning to must, have to, should, ought to in English.) This means the same with '-아/어/여야 되다' but in spoken language '되다' is more often used.

When the final vowel of the verb stem is 'ㅏ' or 'ㅗ', it takes '-아야 하다'.

When the final vowel of the verb stem is other than 'ㅏ' or 'ㅗ', it takes '-어야 하다'. When combined with the verbs ending with '하다', it makes either '하여야 하다' or '해야 하다'. In spoken Korean, '해야 하다' is more often used.

> 예문 지금 꼭 가야 해요? Do you have to go now?
>
> 수수료를 내셔야 합니다. You must pay the commission.
>
> 내일까지 숙제를 해야 해요.
> You must hand in your assignment by tomorrow.

2. -(으)려고 하다

'-(으)려고 하다' indicates the speaker's intention or will. '-으려고 하다' is attached to the verb stem ending in a consonant, and '-려고 하다' is attached to the verb stem ending in a vowel.

> 예문 배가 고파서 점심을 먹으려고 해요.
> I am hungry, so I am going to have lunch.
>
> 지나 씨는 친구 생일 선물을 하나 사려고 합니다.
> Jina is going to buy a birthday present for her friend.
>
> 중국에 돈을 보내려고 하는데요.
> I would like to wire some money to China.

••• Practice

Look at the picture below and practice the conversation as suggested by the following example.

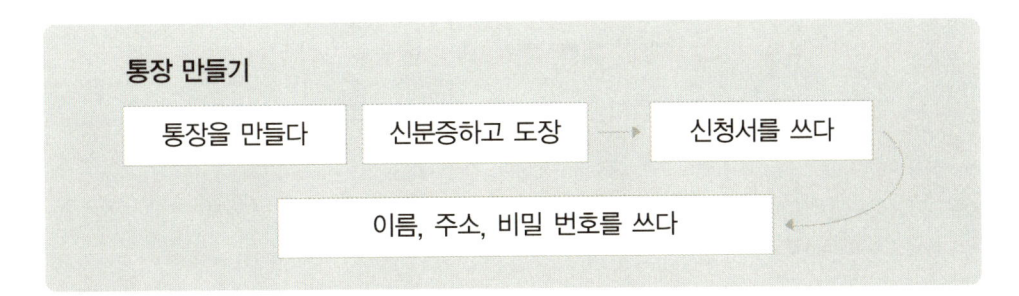

통장 만들기

통장을 만들다 → 신분증하고 도장 → 신청서를 쓰다

이름, 주소, 비밀 번호를 쓰다

> 보기
> 은행원: 뭘 도와 드릴까요?
> 손 님: 통장을 만들려고 하는데요.
> 은행원: 그럼 신분증하고 도장을 주시겠어요?
> 손 님: 여기 있어요.
> 은행원: 신청서를 쓰셔야 하는데요.
>   여기에 이름, 주소, 비밀 번호를 써 주세요.
> 손 님: 알겠습니다.

① **돈 찾기**

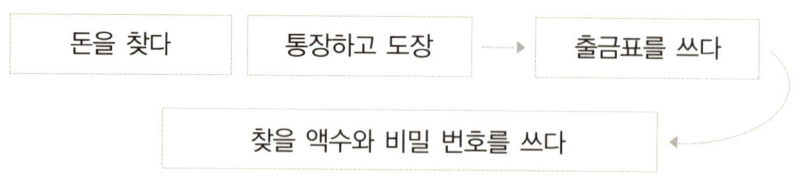

　　돈을 찾다 → 통장하고 도장 → 출금표를 쓰다 → 찾을 액수와 비밀 번호를 쓰다

② **환전하기**

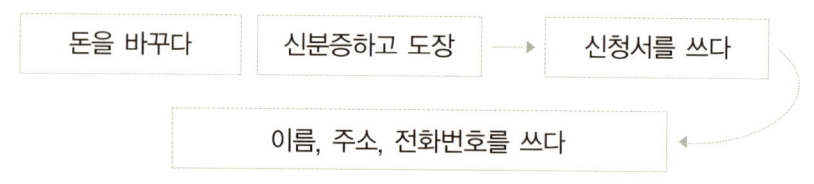

　　돈을 바꾸다 → 신분증하고 도장 → 신청서를 쓰다 → 이름, 주소, 전화번호를 쓰다

③ **카드 만들기**

　　카드를 만들다 → 신분증하고 도장 → 신청서를 쓰다 → 이름, 주소, 비밀 번호를 쓰다

출금표 withdrawal slip

Bank 은행

> >>> Korean Culture

A person with Korean citizenship will be given 'a residence card' when he/she becomes 17 years old. It is an official identification card, which is essential in one's daily life in Korea. The card is needed to open a bank account or to make a contract and many more.

Pronunciation

Listen and repeat.

1. 읽어요.
2. 앉으세요.
3. 밟아요.
4. 삶아요.

>>> Talk 1

You are trying to exchange the local currency. Please check the exchange rate and exchange your country's currency for Korean currency, using roll cards.

Ⓐ
1) 어서 오십시오.
3) _____ 달러(마르크, 프랑, 원…)에 _____ 원입니다.
5) 네. 수표로 드릴까요, 아니면 현금으로 드릴까요?
7) 수수료는 없습니다.

Ⓑ
2) _____을/를 바꾸려고 하는데요.
  오늘 환율이 어떻게 되지요?
4) 이 돈을 한국 돈으로 바꿔 주세요.
6) 현금으로 주세요. 수수료는 얼마예요?

수표 check   현금 cash   바꾸다 to exchange

>>> Talk 2

What kinds of services do banks provide in your country? Please explain them comparing services provided by Korean banks.

한국

· 출금할 수 있어요.
· 입금할 수 있어요.
· 송금할 수 있어요.
· 환전할 수 있어요.
· 신용카드를 만들어요.
· 주식 투자를 해요.

〈여러분 나라〉

주식 투자 investment in stocks

>>> Korean Culture

Tourists can trade their native currency in the airports, banks or money exchange booths. Foreign tourists with valid passports can exchange up to USD10,000 if he/she stays in one country for more than 6 months.

>>> Talk 3

Nowadays, many Koreans use phone-banking and Internet-banking service instead of going to a bank. Practice the conversation by comparing Korea and your country in terms of banking services as the following example suggests.

> 보기
> - 현금 인출기로도 송금할 수 있어요.
> - 카드 비밀 번호와 돈을 받을 사람의 계좌 번호를 알아야 해요.
> - 은행에 가지 않고 송금할 수 있어서 편리해요.

현금 인출기 ATM(Automated Teller Machine)   편리하다 to be convenient

>>> Check Yourself

Evaluate your own improvement after studying this chapter.

	Poor	Fair	Good
I can deposit money at the bank.			
I can withdraw money from the bank.			
I can send money from one bank to another.			

Lesson 17 | Illness
병

••• Goals

- **Tasks:** Talking about symptoms, Making recommendations to someone who is sick
- **Grammar:** -(으)ㄴ 것 같다
  -는 것 같다
  -(으)ㄹ 것 같다
- **Vocabulary & Expressions:** Illness-related vocabulary
- **Pronunciation:** Tensification 4
- **Korean Culture:** A herb doctor clinic

>>> Get Ready

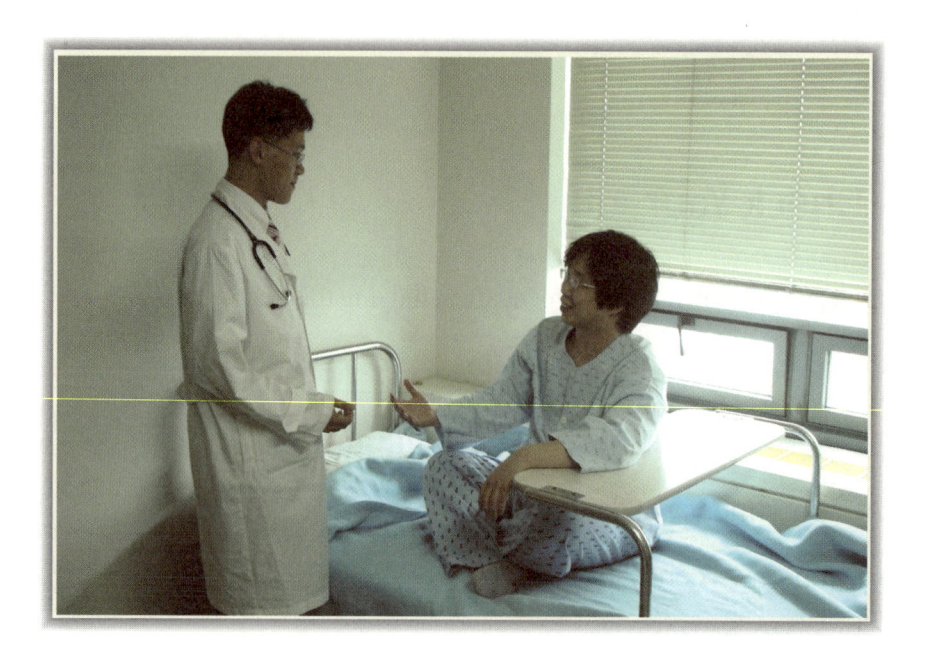

Who works in this place?
When do you go to this place?

Illness 병

••• Listen

Listen to the following conversation and repeat.

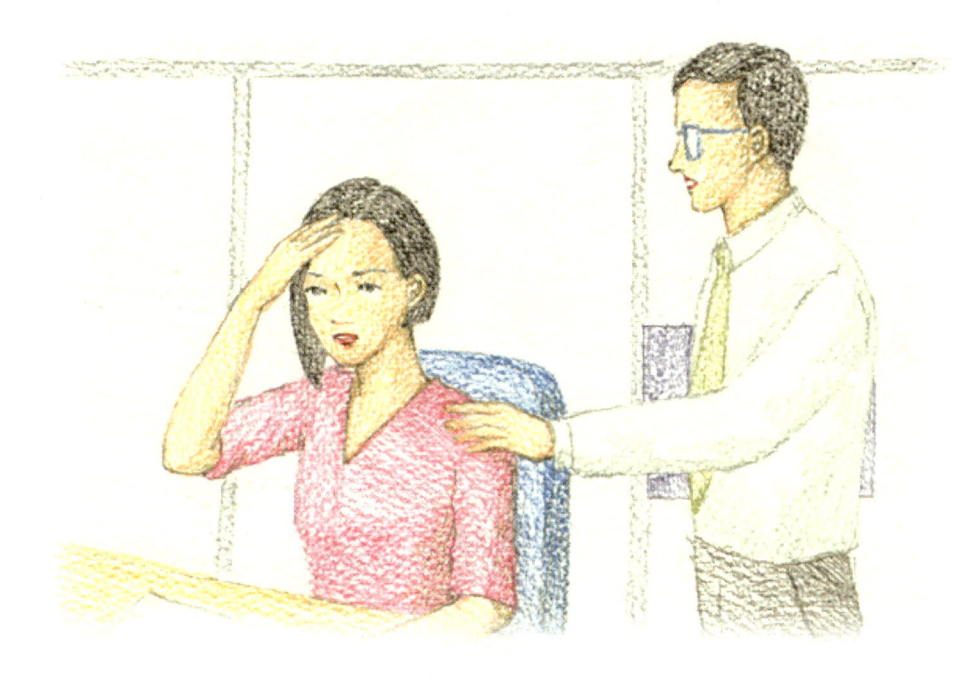

이영수 : 미정 씨, 어디 아프세요?
김미정 : 네, 조금 전부터 열이 나고 머리가 아파요.
　　　　감기에 걸린 것 같아요.
이영수 : 병원에 가 보셨어요?
김미정 : 아니요, 그래서 오늘은 일찍 퇴근해야 할 것 같아요.
이영수 : 어서 병원에 가 보세요.
김미정 : 죄송해요. 그럼, 먼저 들어갈게요.

어서 right away, with haste　　　　퇴근하다 to get off and go home from work

••• Vocabulary

Vocabulary plays an important role in speaking fluent Korean. Check out the following words.

열이 나다	기침이 나다	머리가 아프다
이가 아프다	배가 아프다	목이 붓다
감기에 걸리다	몸살이 나다	눈이 충혈되다

Illness 병

> **>>> Korean Culture**
>
> As folk remedies, Koreans use traditional herbal medicines for minor illness such as cold. When a Korean comes down with flu, he/she can fix the problem by having the following food.
> * bean sprout soup with red pepper powder
> * ginger extract with honey in warm water
> * roots of garlic
> * warm tea with dried orange peel
> * lemon preserved in sugar
> * pear extract

>>> Speak

••• Grammar

Grammar is also an important factor in speaking Korean fluently. Look at the following grammar points.

-(으)ㄴ 것 같다, -는 것 같다, -(으)ㄹ 것 같다

This pattern indicates the conjecture of the speaker. It takes different forms depending on whether something occurred in the past, is occurring in the present, or will occur in the future.

[현재] -(으)ㄴ/는 것 같다

'-는 것 같다' is attached to the stem of the verbs and '있다/없다' to indicate the conjecture of the speaker on what is occurring now. In case of the adjective, '-(으)ㄴ 것 같다' is attached to the adjective stem.

예문 비가 오는 것 같아요. It seems to rain.

영화가 재미있는 것 같아요. 사람들이 많아요.
    The movie seems interesting. There are a lot of people.

수미 씨 생각이 좋은 것 같아요. Sumi's idea seems good.

165

[과거] −(으)ㄴ 것 같다

Attached to the verb stem, it indicates the conjecture of the speaker on what occurred in the past.

예문 벌써 비가 그친 것 같아요. It seems that the rain stopped already.

민수는 이미 점심을 먹은 것 같아요.
　　　It seems that Minsu already had lunch.

시몽 씨는 벌써 떠난 것 같아요. 전화를 안 받아요.
　　　It seems that Simon has already left. No one answers the phone.

cf. '−았/었/였던 것 같아요' is attached to the stem of adjectives and '있다/없다' to express a conjecture of the speaker on the past event.

영화가 재미있었던 것 같아요.
　　　I guess the movie was interesting.

어제 학교에 사람이 많았던 것 같아요.
　　　I guess there were many people in the school yesterday.

[미래] −(으)ㄹ 것 같다

Attached to the stem of the verb, the adjective, and '있다/없다', it indicates the conjecture of the speaker.

예문 비가 올 것 같아요. It seems that it will rain.

민수는 곧 점심을 먹을 것 같아요.
　　　It seems that Minsu will have lunch soon.

영희 씨 딸도 예쁠 것 같아요.
　　　I guess Yeonghui's daughter is pretty too.

한국어 배울 거예요. 재미있을 것 같아요.
　　　I am going to learn Korean. It seems that I will have fun.

Illness 병

••• Practice

Look at the picture below and practice the conversation as suggested by the following example.

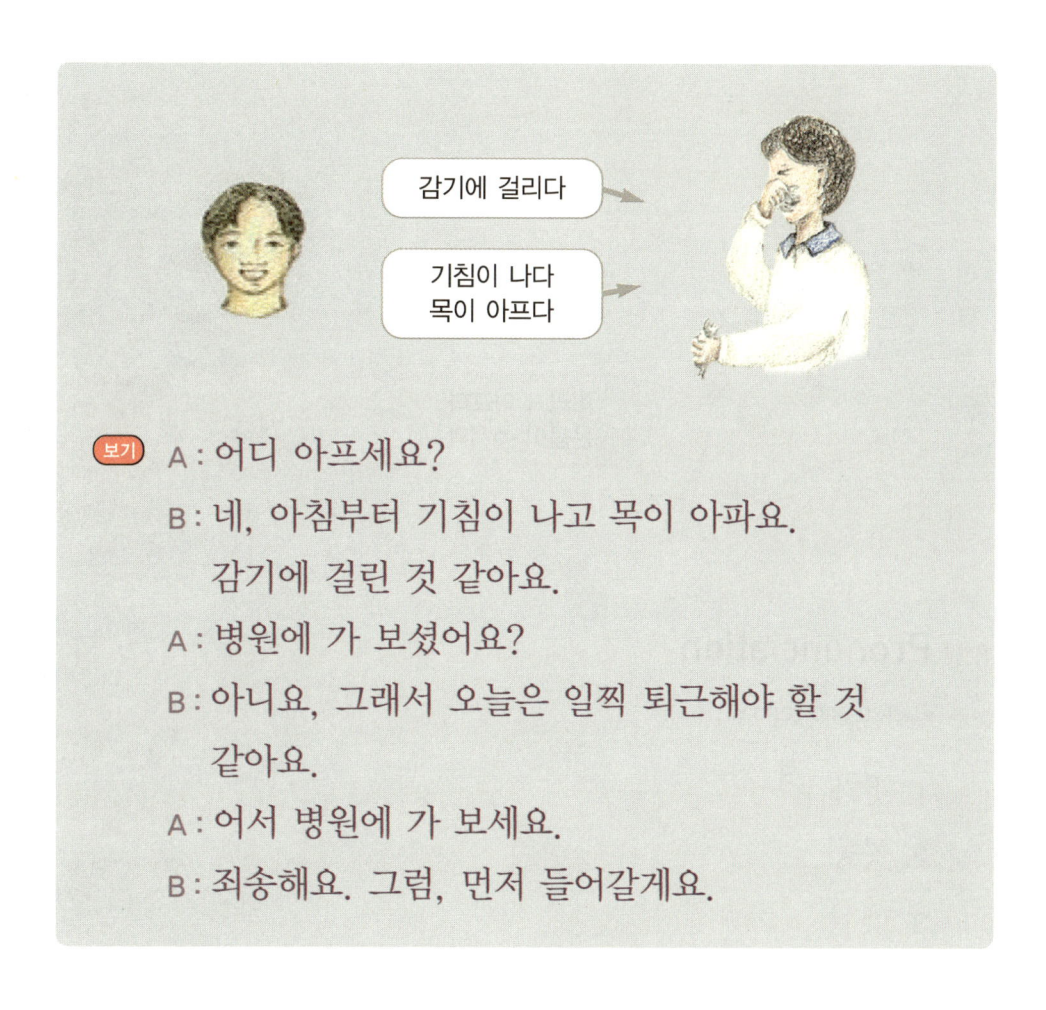

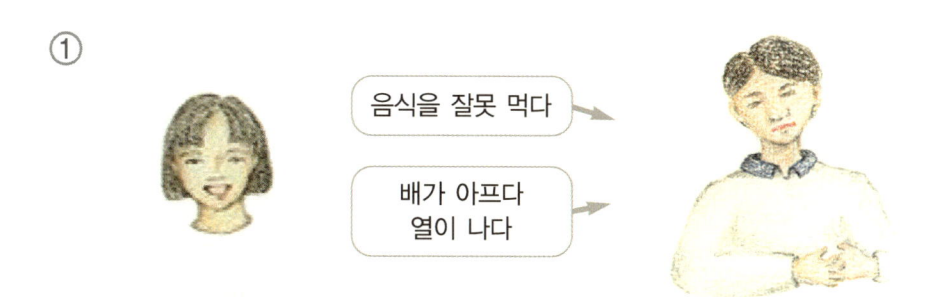

감기에 걸리다

기침이 나다
목이 아프다

보기 A : 어디 아프세요?
B : 네, 아침부터 기침이 나고 목이 아파요.
감기에 걸린 것 같아요.
A : 병원에 가 보셨어요?
B : 아니요, 그래서 오늘은 일찍 퇴근해야 할 것 같아요.
A : 어서 병원에 가 보세요.
B : 죄송해요. 그럼, 먼저 들어갈게요.

①

음식을 잘못 먹다

배가 아프다
열이 나다

167

② 눈병에 걸리다
눈이 따갑다
눈이 충혈되었다

③ 몸살이 나다
머리가 아프다
온몸이 쑤시다

••• Pronunciation

Listen and repeat.

1. 냇가
2. 콧등
3. 햇살
4. 깃발

>>> Talk 1

Let's role-play. Your role is to explain symptoms as the example shows and your partner's role is to tell the name of the illness among the following choices.

Illness 병

감기 독감 몸살
배탈 식중독 눈병 치통

보기 〈감기〉
목이 붓고 기침이 많이 나요.
콧물도 조금 나고 머리도 조금 아파요.
몸이 쑤시지는 않아요.

>>> Korean Culture

Koreans often go to 'Oriental medicine clinic's when they are sick. Oriental medicine focuses on figuring out the origin of the illness, rebalancing the elements in one's body, and taking a holistic approach towards one's health. Oriental medical doctors prescribe 'herbal medicine' made from a variety of herb, bear's gall bladders, young antlers of a deer and etc. This herbal medicine helps to develop the patient's stamina or cure a disease.

>>> **Talk 2**

The followings are the medicines you are able to purchase from Korean drugstores. Please explain the symptoms as the example shows and buy an appropriate medicine.

증상	필요한 약
머리가 아프다.	두통약
손을 베었다.	소독약, 밴드
배가 아프다.	소화제

> 보기
> A : 어서 오세요. 뭘 드릴까요?
> B : 저, 머리가 아픈데요.
> A : 아, 두통약이 필요하세요?
> B : 네, 두통약 좀 주세요.
> A : 이걸 드셔 보세요.

증상 symptom　　두통약 pain relief　　소독약 disinfectant　　소화제 digestive
베다 to cut

>>> Talk 3

Fill in the blanks below and talk as the following example suggests.

Illness 병

왜 아팠습니까?	감기	
언제 아팠습니까?	지난 가을	
얼마 동안 아팠습니까?	한 달	
어떻게 아팠습니까?	기침, 열	
어떻게 했습니까?	병원에 가다, 약, 주사	

보기 저는 지난 가을에 감기에 걸려서 많이 아팠어요.
한 달 동안 낫지 않았어요.
기침이 많이 나고 열도 많이 났어요.
병원에 가서 약도 먹고 주사도 맞았어요.

동안 for/during　　(감기) 주사 맞다 to get a (flu) shot

>>> Check Yourself

Evaluate your own improvement after studying this chapter.

	Poor	Fair	Good
I can explain the symptoms.			
I can give recommendations to someone who is sick.			

Lesson 18 Weather
날씨

●●● Goals
- **Tasks:** Talking about weather
- **Grammar:** -겠- 2
  -기 전에
- **Vocabulary & Expressions:** Season and weather-related vocabulary
- **Pronunciation:** Liquid
- **Korean Culture:** Four seasons

>>> Get Ready

How is the weather today?
What would you like to do in this kind of weather?

Weather 날씨

••• Listen

Listen to the following conversation and repeat.

김미정: 오늘 날씨가 흐리네요.
이영수: 네, 곧 비가 올 것 같아요.
김미정: 비가 오면 길이 더 막히겠지요?
이영수: 그렇겠죠? 오늘은 막히기 전에 퇴근해야겠어요.
김미정: 저도 지금 퇴근하려고요.

흐리다 to be cloudy   (교통이) 막히다 traffic is conjested

••• Vocabulary

Vocabulary plays an important role in speaking fluent Korean. Check out the following words.

봄	여름	가을	겨울
덥다	춥다	맑다	비가 오다
소나기가 오다	바람이 불다	구름이 끼다	안개가 끼다
눈이 오다	흐리다	쌀쌀하다	후텁지근하다

Weather 날씨

> **>>> Korean Culture**
>
> You can experience all four seasons in Korea. It gets warmer and flowers bloom when spring begins in early March. In addition, sandy dust from China affects many parts of Korea and it rains frequently in most of the places during spring. During the summer mouths from June to August, it is hot and humid. During the rainy season in summer, it often rains very heavily in most parts of Korea. After the heat of summer fades away, people can enjoy a crisp blue sky and moderate weather in autumn. Winter starts from late November and lasts until early March. During winter, Korea gets a lot of snow due to the cold continental high atmospheric pressure from Siberia.

>>> Speak

••• Grammar

Grammar is also an important factor in speaking Korean fluently. Look at the following grammar points.

1. -겠- 2

'-겠-' is used to construct the future tense and indicates conjecture, a person's intention, or possibility. In this lesson '-겠-' is used to indicate the conjecture of the speaker in statements.

> (예문) 내일은 날씨가 흐리겠습니다. It will be cloudy tomorrow.
>
> 시험 준비 때문에 바쁘겠어요. You must be busy preparing the exam.
>
> 비가 오면 퇴근 시간에 길이 복잡하겠어요.
>   If it rains, there will be a traffic jam during rush hour.

2. -기 전에

'-기 전에' is attached to a verb stem to give the meaning of 'before'.

예문 가기 전에 전화하세요. Please call me before you go.

저녁을 먹기 전에 손을 씻어요. I wash my hands before I eat dinner.

자기 전에 일기를 써요. I write my diary before I sleep.

••• Practice

Look at the picture below and practice the conversation as suggested by the following example.

덥다
소나기가 오다

보기 A : 오늘 날씨가 덥네요.
B : 네, 곧 소나기가 올 것 같아요.
A : 소나기가 오면 길이 더 막히겠지요?
B : 그렇겠죠? 길 막히기 전에 퇴근해야겠어요.
A : 저도 지금 퇴근하려고요.

① 흐리다
비가 오다

② 구름이 많이 끼었다
눈이 오다

Weather 날씨

③

후텁지근하다
비가 오다

••• **Pronunciation**

Listen and repeat.

1. 난로
2. 대관령
3. 전라도
4. 줄넘기

>>> **Talk 1**

What are you able to do if the weather condition is like as described in the following table? And what would you like to do? Please fill in the table and talk about them after you talk with your partner.

날씨	할 수 있는 것	하고 싶은 것
비가 오다		
눈이 오다		
날씨가 맑다		

177

>>> Talk 2

Please talk about the seasons and weather of your country.

계절	날씨

>>> Talk 3

The followings are the weather forecasts for several cities. Talk about the weather in each city as the following example suggests.

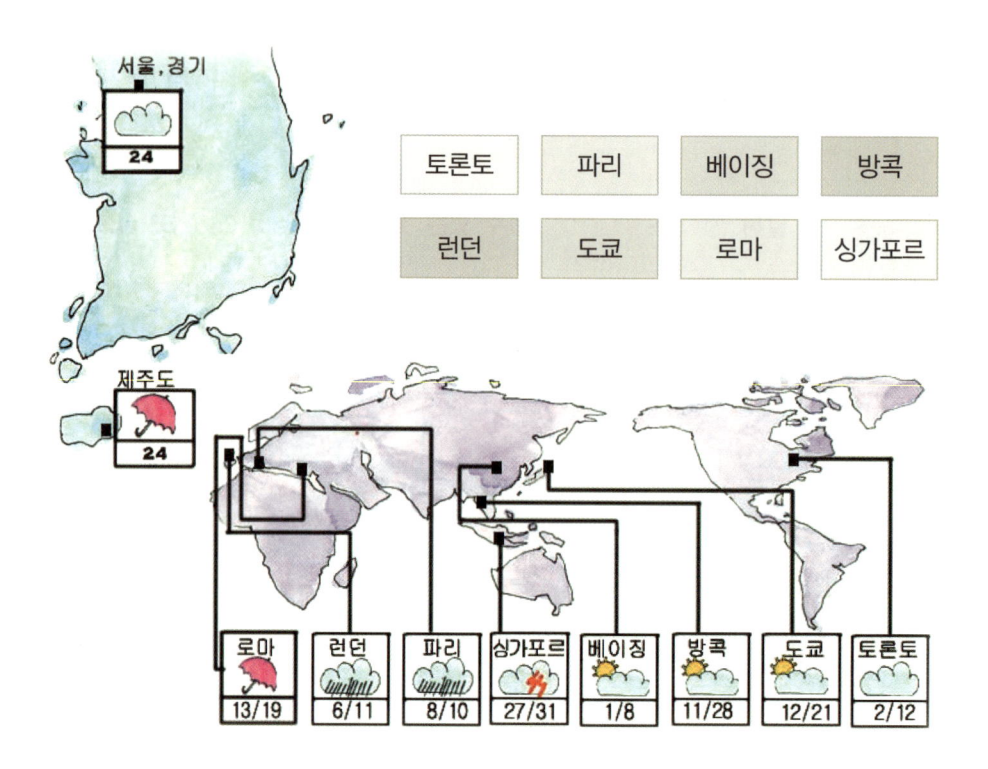

| 토론토 | 파리 | 베이징 | 방콕 |
| 런던 | 도쿄 | 로마 | 싱가포르 |

서울, 경기 24
제주도 24
로마 13/19
런던 6/11
파리 8/10
싱가포르 27/31
베이징 1/8
방콕 11/28
도쿄 12/21
토론토 2/12

Weather 날씨

> 보기 A: 서울 날씨가 어때요?
> B: 서울은 구름이 끼고 흐려요.
> A: 베이징 날씨는 어때요?
> B: 베이징 날씨는 맑은 후에 조금 흐려지겠습니다.

서울 날씨가 어때요? What is the weather like in Seoul?

>>> Check Yourself

Evaluate your own improvement after studying this chapter.

	Poor	Fair	Good
I can talk about the seasons.			
I can talk about the weather.			

맑음 　　　구름 　　　비 　　　눈

179

Lesson 19 | Travel 여행

••• Goals
- **Tasks:** Making a reservation, Making travel plans
- **Grammar:** -(으)로 2
  -(으)려면
- **Vocabulary & Expressions:** Vocabulary related to reservations
- **Pronunciation:** Intonation of a choice-question
- **Korean Culture:** Tourist Information, Airport

>>> Get Ready

Have you ever booked a flight through a travel agent?
Where do you want to travel to?

••• Listen

Listen to the following conversation and repeat.

(여행사에서)

이영수 : 17일에 홍콩 가는 비행기 표를 예매하고 싶은데요.
　　　　대한 항공을 예약할 수 있습니까?

직　원 : 17일에 출발하시려면 아시아나 항공을
　　　　이용하셔야 합니다. 괜찮으시겠습니까?

이영수 : 네, 그렇게 하겠습니다.
　　　　17일에 떠나서 21일에 도착할 수 있습니까?

직　원 : 잠깐만 기다리십시오.
　　　　(조금 후에)

직　원 : 17일에 출발, 21일에 서울 도착하는 비행기 표가
　　　　예약되었습니다. 계산은 현금으로 하시겠습니까?
　　　　카드로 하시겠습니까?

이영수 : 현금으로 하겠습니다.

••• Vocabulary

Vocabulary plays an important role in speaking fluent Korean. Check out the following words.

여행	travel	도착하다	to depart
여행지	destination	출발하다	to arrive
숙소	place to stay	예매하다	to book
3박 4일	3 nights and 4 days	예약하다	to reserve
일정	Schedule		
예상경비	expected cost		

> **>>> Korean Culture**
>
> You can get useful travel information on Korea from tourist information centers or any guide center affiliated with the Ministry of Culture and Tourism. Guide maps and brochures in English, Japanese and Chinese are available along with the help from the staff, fluent in many foreign languages. The office hours are usually from 9:00 am to 5:00~6:00 pm. For further information on travel to Korea, log on to (http://english.tour2korea.com)

>>> Speak

••• Grammar

Grammar is also an important factor in speaking Korean fluently. Look at the following grammar points.

Travel **여행**

1. -(으)로 2

'-(으)로' is attached to a noun indicating an instrument or means to do something with, and expresses the meaning of '~를 가지고 (with)'. After the name of transportation, it means '~을 이용하여 (by)' or '~을 가지고 (with)'. '-으로' is attached to a noun ending in a consonant, and '-로' is attached to a noun ending in a vowel.

> **예문** 계산은 현금으로 하시겠습니까? Are you going to pay in cash?
>
> 인터넷으로 정보를 찾아보세요. Find some information on the Internet.
>
> 서울에서는 지하철로 어디든지 갈 수 있습니다.
> You can go anywhere by subway in Seoul.

2. -(으)려면

'-(으)려면' is translated as 'if you intend to' or 'if you are to'. '-으려면' is attached to the verb stem ending in a consonant, and '-려면' is attached to the verb stem ending in a vowel.

> **예문** 늦지 않으려면 일찍 떠나야 해요.
> If you are not to be late, you should leave early.
>
> 물건을 싸게 사려면 남대문 시장에 가야 해요.
> If you are to buy things at good prices, you should go to Namdaemun Market.
>
> 시험을 잘 보려면 열심히 공부하십시오.
> If you are to get a good grade, study hard.

••• Practice

Look at the picture below and practice the conversation as suggested by the following example.

6일/뉴욕/7박 8일/카드

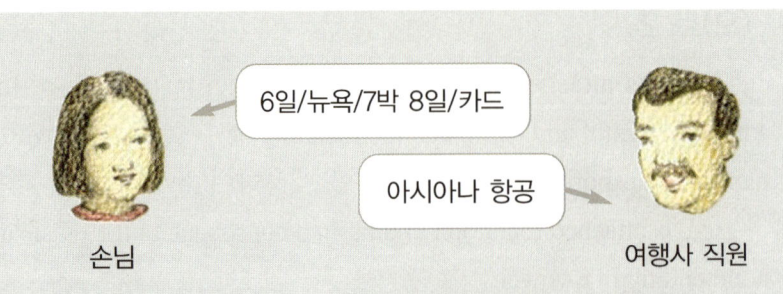

아시아나 항공

손님   여행사 직원

보기 (여행사에서)

손님 : 6일에 뉴욕 가는 비행기 표를 예매하고
　　　싶은데요.
직원 : 아시아나 항공으로 가시겠습니까?
손님 : 그러죠. 7박 8일 여행을 가려고 하는데요.
직원 : 잠깐만 기다리십시오.
　　　(조금 후에)
직원 : 손님, 6일 출발, 13일 서울 도착하는
　　　비행기 표가 예약되었습니다.
　　　계산은 현금으로 하시겠습니까?
　　　카드로 하시겠습니까?
손님 : 카드로 하겠습니다. 여기요.
직원 : 고맙습니다. 즐거운 여행 되십시오.

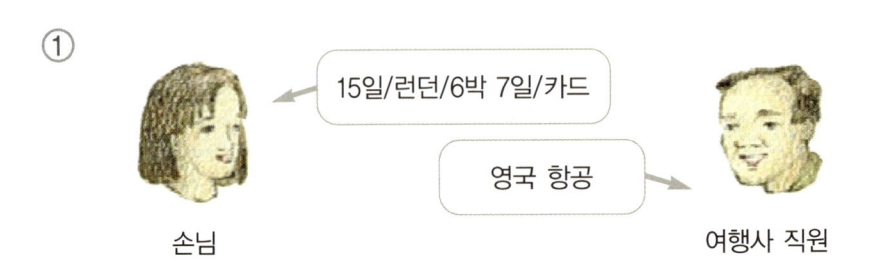

①

15일/런던/6박 7일/카드

영국 항공

손님   여행사 직원

Travel 여행

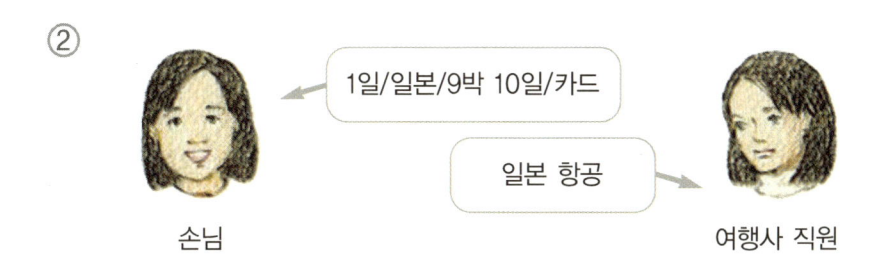

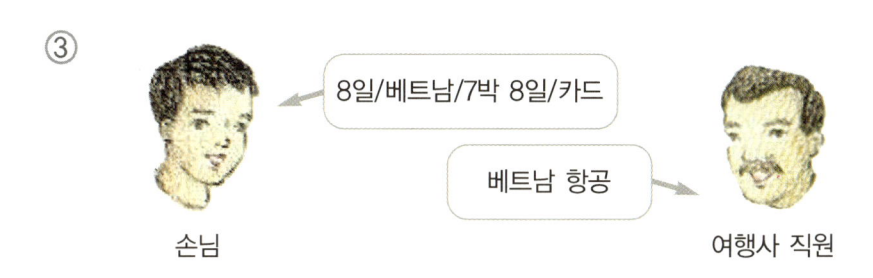

②
손님 ← 1일/일본/9박 10일/카드
여행사 직원 → 일본 항공

③
손님 ← 8일/베트남/7박 8일/카드
여행사 직원 → 베트남 항공

••• Pronunciation

Listen and repeat.

1. 계산은 현금으로 하시겠습니까? 카드로 하시겠습니까?
2. 음악회에 갈까요? 극장에 갈까요?
3. 저녁은 지금 먹을래요? 이따가 먹을래요?

>>> Talk 1

You are planning to travel Japan for 3 nights and 4 days. Please refer to the table and make a reservation as the example shows.

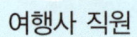

	가격	27일(목)		28일(금)		29일(토)		30일(일)		31일(월)	
		서울→도쿄	도쿄→서울	서울→도쿄	도쿄→서울	서울→도쿄	도쿄→서울	서울→도쿄	도쿄→서울	서울→도쿄	도쿄→서울
대한 항공 (KA)	536,800원	O	×	×	O	O	O	O	O	O	×
아시아나 항공 (Asiana)	480,000원	×	×	O	×	×	O	O	×	×	O
일본 항공 (JAL)	450,000원	O	O	×	O	×	×	O	×	×	O

보기 손님: 3박 4일로 도쿄에 여행을 가려고 하는데요.

직원: 언제 출발하세요?

손님: 10월 28일에 출발해요.

Travel 여행

> 직원: 10월 28일에 도쿄에 가는 비행기는 아시아나 항공이 있습니다.
> 10월 31일에 인천공항에 오는 비행기도 아시아나 항공이 있습니다.
> 손님: 가격이 어떻게 됩니까?
> 직원: 왕복 480,000원입니다.
> 손님: 네.

왕복 round trip

>>> Korean Culture

There are 3 international airports (i.e. Incheon, Busan and Jeju) and 13 domestic airports in Korea. In Incheon Airport, there are services from 35 reputable international airlines, including Korean Air and Asiana Airlines.

>>> Talk 2

Work with a partner and plan a vacation with him/her.

여행지 (destination)	여행 기간 (duration)	숙소 (place to stay)	누구와 같이 (with whom)	여행지에서 할 일 (things to do)	예상 경비 (expected cost)
제주도	3박 4일	호텔	친구	한라산 해변 관광	70만 원

보기
A: 이번 휴가에 어디로 가면 좋을까요?
B: 글쎄요.
A: 제주도 어때요?
B: 좋아요. 그런데 제주도는 뭐로 유명해요?
A: 아름다운 자연으로 유명해요.
한라산과 해변이 특히 아름다워요.
B: 그래요? 비용은 얼마나 들어요?
A: 호텔에서 숙박하면 4일에 70만 원쯤 들 거예요.
B: 그럼, 제주도로 갑시다.

여행지 (destination)	여행 기간 (duration)	숙소 (place to stay)	누구와 같이 (with whom)	여행지에서 할 일 (things to do)	예상 경비 (expected cost)

유명하다 to be famous   비용 cost   해변 beach   숙박 lodging

>>> Talk 3

Introduce the famous tourist attractions in your country as the following example suggests.

> **보기** 부산은 한국에서 두 번째로 큰 도시입니다.
> 시원한 바다가 있어서 여름에 가면 참 좋습니다.
> 해운대는 부산에서 유명한 해수욕장입니다.
> 경치가 아주 좋습니다.
> 부산에 가면 회를 꼭 드셔 보세요.
> 싱싱하고 맛이 좋고 값도 쌉니다.

| 회 Sashimi | 싱싱하다 to be fresh | 해수욕장 swimming beach |

>>> Check Yourself

Evaluate your own improvement after studying this chapter.

	Poor	Fair	Good
I can make reservations.			
I can make travel plans.			

Lesson 20 | Lodging
숙박

••• Goals

- **Tasks:** Using lodging facilities
- **Grammar:** −(으)면 되다
  −아/어/여 주시겠어요?
- **Vocabulary & Expressions:** Vocabulary related to using lodging facilities
- **Pronunciation:** Pronunciation of '의'
- **Korean Culture:** *Minbak, Ondol*

>>> Get Ready

Can you name these places?
Where is the best place to stay?

••• Listen

Listen to the following conversation and repeat.

주   인 : 방이 마음에 드십니까?

톰 스미스 : 네, 그런데 좀 덥네요.

주   인 : 저기 에어컨을 켜시면 됩니다.

톰 스미스 : 그래요? 참, 내일 여섯 시에 좀 깨워 주시겠어요?

주   인 : 네, 알겠습니다. 또 뭐 불편하신 점은 없으세요?

톰 스미스 : 없습니다.

깨우다 to wake up

●●● Vocabulary

Vocabulary plays an important role in speaking fluent Korean. Check out the following words.

호텔	hotel	여관	inn
콘도	timeshare	펜션	pension
민박	providing bed and meals	온돌방	under floor-heating room
욕실	bathroom	침실	bedroom
에어컨	air conditioner	히터	heater
이불	bedclothes	베개	pillow
온수	hot water	잠그다	to lock
마음에 들다	to like, to enjoy	켜다	to turn on
끄다	to turn off		

> >>> Korean Culture
>
> Foreign tourists can experience a Korean homestay called '민박'. Although it may not be as comfortable as hotels or timeshares, it offers an unique opportunity to experience Korean culture and custom while living with a Korean family. For more information on 민박, you may visit the websites.

>>> Speak

●●● Grammar

Grammar is also an important factor in speaking Korean fluently. Look at the following grammar points.

1. -(으)면 되다

'-(으)면 되다' is used when we talk about a simple or easy solution. '되다'

means in this pattern 'to be enough'. '–으면 되다' is attached to the verb stem ending in a consonant other than 'ㄹ', and '–면 되다' is attached to the verb stem ending in a vowel and 'ㄹ'.

> **예문** 머리가 아플 때 저는 이 약을 먹으면 됩니다.
> Take the medicine when you have a headache, and it will help (ease your pain).
>
> 더울 때는 저 에어컨을 켜면 됩니다.
> Turn on the air conditioner when you feel hot, and it will help.
>
> 피곤할 때는 잠을 푹 자면 됩니다.
> When feeling tired, a sound sleep will help.

2. –아/어/여 주시겠어요?

'–아/어/여 주시겠어요?' is used to make a request or to ask for help. Since this pattern takes the form of the question, it sounds politer, making the listener feel less burdensome. If you use this pattern with '좀' in front of it, it feels even politer.

> **예문** 저 좀 도와주시겠어요? Would you help me please?
>
> 사진 좀 찍어 주시겠어요? Would you take a photo please?
>
> 문 좀 열어 주시겠어요? Would you open the door please?

••• Practice

Look at the picture below and practice the conversation as suggested by the following example.

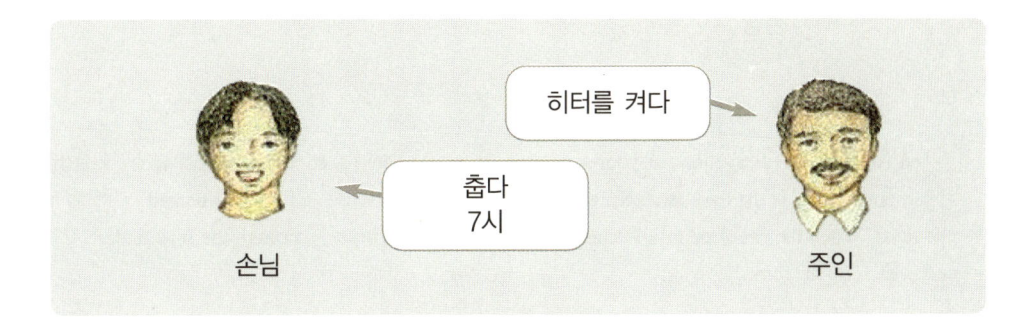

히터를 켜다

춥다
7시

손님   주인

보기 주인: 방이 마음에 드세요?
손님: 네, 그런데 좀 추워요.
주인: 히터를 켜시면 돼요.
손님: 그래요? 고맙습니다.
       내일 7시에 깨워 주시겠어요?
주인: 네, 알겠습니다. 뭐 불편하신 점은 없으세요?
손님: 없습니다.

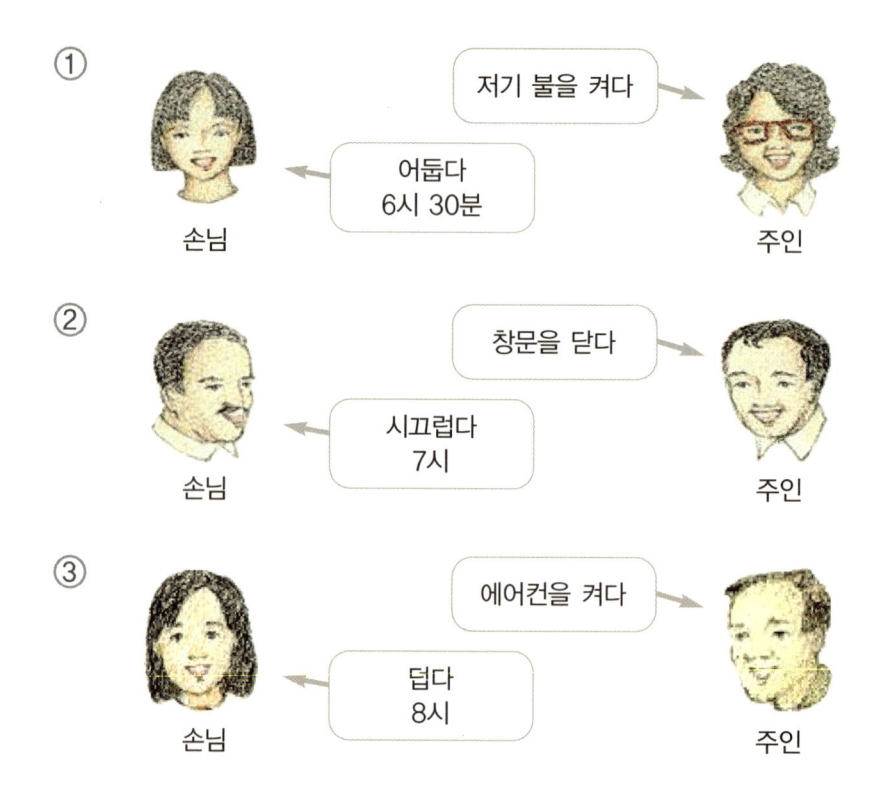

① 손님 ← 어둡다 6시 30분 / 저기 불을 켜다 → 주인

② 손님 ← 시끄럽다 7시 / 창문을 닫다 → 주인

③ 손님 ← 덥다 8시 / 에어컨을 켜다 → 주인

>>> Korean Culture

When you make a reservation for your accommodation, you are asked to choose between '온돌방' and 'bedroom'. '온돌' is the traditional Korean heating system which uses a flat stone named '구들장' under the floor. When the fireplace in a kitchen is heated, the hot air moves through the pipe under '구들장' and warms up the room.

••• Pronunciation

Listen and repeat.

1. 의사
2. 회의
3. 언니의 책

>>> Talk 1

Let's role-play. Your role is a hotel employee and your partner's role is a customer. Please ask and respond as the example shows.

예약자	인원	숙박일
김수미	4인	3박
이영민	5인	6박
박수민	2인	5박

보기
A: 저 예약한 사람인데요.
B: 성함이 어떻게 되세요?
A: 김수미입니다.
B: 네. 김수미 씨, 4인, 3박 예약하셨죠?
A: 네, 그래요.
B: 방 번호는 513호실입니다. 여기 열쇠 받으시고요. 여기 있는 서류를 작성해 주세요.
A: 네, 알겠습니다.

>>> Talk 2

Please refer to the tables below and talk about good points of accommodations you like as the example shows.

	좋은 점	나쁜 점
콘도	· 값이 싸다 · 요리를 할 수 있다	· 날마다 청소를 해 주는 서비스가 없다 · 시설이 좋지는 않다
호텔	· 날마다 청소를 해주는 서비스가 있다 · 침대, 가구 등 시설이 아주 깨끗하고 좋다	· 값이 비싸다 · 요리를 할 수 없다

보기
A : 저는 콘도가 좋다고 생각해요.
값도 싸고 요리도 할 수 있어요.
그리도 친구들과 같이 잘 수 있어서 좋아요.
콘도에서 같이 자면 정말 재미있어요.
B : 저는 콘도도 좋지만 호텔이 더 좋다고 생각해요.
콘도에서 자면, 직접 청소해야 돼요.
여행까지 와서 청소를 하고 싶지 않아요.
호텔은 서비스와 시설이 좋아요.
값이 비싸지만 편안하게 여행을 즐길 수 있어요.

	좋은 점	나쁜 점
민박		
여관		

>>> Talk 3

The followings are the types of Korean accommodations. Then, please talk about whether you have similar types of accommodations in your country.

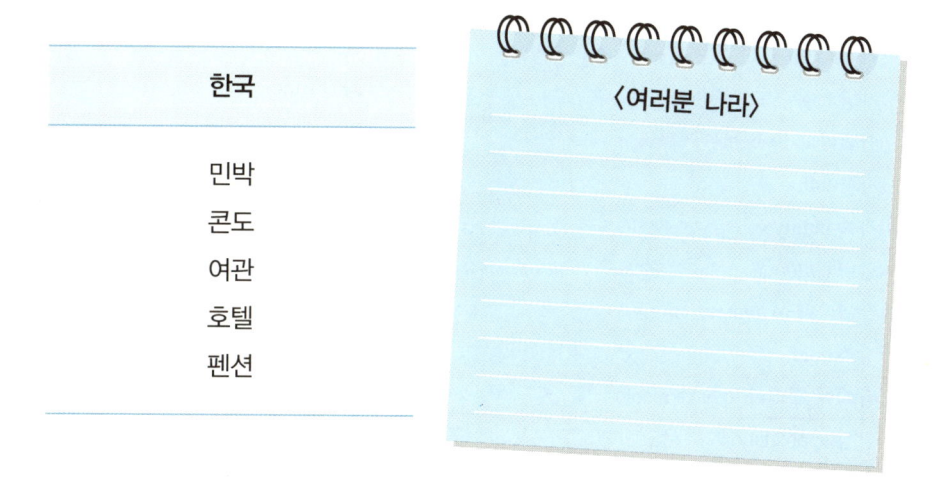

한국
민박
콘도
여관
호텔
펜션

〈여러분 나라〉

>>> Check Yourself

Evaluate your own improvement after studying this chapter.

	Poor	Fair	Good
I can use lodging facilities.			
I can ask for favors and information while traveling.			

Index

ㄱ

가구 furniture	196
가다 to go	101
가방 bag	120
가볍다 to be light	119
가을 fall	174
가족 family	45
갈비 *Galbi*	88
갈아타다 to transfer	101
감기 cold	163
감기에 걸리다 to have a cold	164
감상 appreciation	115
갑자기 suddenly	136
같이 together	63, 109
개 unit of, piece of	37
거기 there	80
거실 living room	28
거울 mirror	26
건강 health	81
건강에 좋다 to be good for health	114
건너 across	91
걷기 walking	102
걸다 to dial	130
걸리다 to take (time)	96
검은색 black color	121
겨울 winter	174
결혼식 wedding ceremony	89
경찰 police	50
계시다 be	147
계좌 번호 an account number	156
고맙다 to thank	97
공연을 보다 to watch a performance	67
공원 park	27, 60
공책 notebook	25
공항 airport	102
과일 fruit	36
과일 가게 fruit shop	42
과자 cookie, sweets	36
괜찮다 to be ok	63
교과서 textbook	43
교실 classroom	28
구 nine	36
구두 shoes	120, 148
구름이 끼다 to be cloudy	174
권 volume	37
그 that	46
그래서 so	78
그럼 well, then	68
그렇지만 but	81
그림 picture, painting	110
극장 theater	27
근처 nearby	125
금요일 Friday	56
기간 period	187
기다리다 to wait	143
기분이 좋다 to feel better	114
기차역 train station	102
기침이 나다 to cough	164
김치 *Gimchi*	81
깨우다 to wake up	191
꽃다발 bouquet	84
끄다 to turn off	192
끼다 to wear (glasses)	149

ㄴ

나 I	47
나라 country	21
나오다 to come out	95
나중에 later	71
낚시 fishing	110
날씨 weather	179
날씬하다 to be slender	148
남동생 younger brother	47
남쪽 the south	92
내리다 to get off	101
내용물 contents	140
내일 tommorow	83
냉면 *Naengmyeon*	74
냉장고 refrigerator	29
네 yes	20
넥타이 tie	148
넷 four	36
노란색 yellow color	121
노래를 부르다 to sing a song	59
노래방 *Noraebang* (commercial singing establishment)	59
녹색 green color	121
녹차 green tea	78
농구 basketball	111
눈병에 걸리다 to have eye infection	168
눈이 오다 to snow	174
눈이 충혈되다 to be bloodshot	164

ㄷ

다니다 to commute, to work	45
다섯 five	36
단정하다 to be net	152
달다 to be sweet	74
달러 dollar	159
대 unit of	37
댁 house	125
덥다 to be hot	174
데이트 date	152
도서관 library	59
도장 seal	156
도착 시간 arrival time	145
도착하다 to arrive	182
도쿄 Tokyo	178
독감 influenza	169
돌아가다 to go back	95
동생 younger brother [sister]	45
동안 for / during	125, 171
동쪽 the east	92
두껍다 to be thick	120
두통약 pain relief	170
둘 two	36
둥글다 to be round	147
뒤 behind, back	26
들다 to eat	73
들어가다 to go in, to go back	163
등산 가다 to climb a mountain	67
등산 mountain climbing	110
따갑다 to be tingling	168
딱딱하다 to be hard	120
딸기 strawberry	78
떡 *Tteok*	78
똑바로 straight	95

뚱뚱하다 to be fat	148		목이 붓다 to have a sore throat	164
			몸살 illness from fatigue	169
			몸살이 나다 to suffer from fatigue	164
## ㄹ			몸이 쑤시다 to feel sharp pains	168
라면 noodles	35		무겁다 to be heavy	121
러시아 Russia	18		무슨 what	22, 71
러시아 사람 Russian	20		문 door	26
런던 London	178		문방구 stationery shop	41
로마 Rome	178		문의하다 to inguire	130
			물 water	39
			뭐 what	29
## ㅁ			뭘 what	73
마리 the number of animals	37		미국 America	18
마음에 들다 to be satisfied	192		미안해요. I'm sorry.	83
막히다 to have a traffic jam	106, 173		미장원 beauty salon	96
만 ten thousands	36		민박 a guest house, homestay room	192
만나다 to meet	63			
만두 dumplings	75			
맑다 to be clear	174		## ㅂ	
맞아요. that's right.	116		바꾸다 to exchange	160
매다 to wear (a necktie)	148		바닷가 the beach	125
맥주 beer	37		바람이 불다 to be windy	174
맵다 to be spicy	74		바지 trousers	120, 150
머리가 아프다 to have a headache	164		밖에 except	119
먹다 to eat	55		밤 night	64
메시지 message	136		밤색 brown color	121
멜론 melon	78		방콕 Bangkok	178
면접 interview	152		방향 direction	105
몇 what	63		배 ship	102
모두 all	35		배 pear	78
모둠회 *Modumhoe*	80		배가 아프다 to have a stomachache	164
모양 shape	119		배낭 backpack	148
모자 hat	124, 148		배우다 to learn	55
목요일 Thursday	56		배탈 stomach upset	169

Korean	English	Page
백	hundred	36
백화점	department store	27
밴드	bandage	170
버스 정류장	bus stop	92, 102
버스	bus	102
번	No.-	104
번호표	number ticket	143
베개	pillow	192
베다	to cut	170
베이징	Beijing	178
변호사	lawyer	50
별 일 없다	not to do anything particular	68
병	bottle of	37
병원	hospital	27
보내다	to send	140
보라색	purple color	121
보통우편	regular mail	139
복잡하다	to be crowded	101
봄	spring	174
봉투	envelope	140
부드럽다	to be soft	120
부산	Busan	189
부인	wife	49
부재중	during[in] one's absence	130
북쪽	the north	92
분	person	147
분	minute	56
분식집	snack corner	77
불고기	Bulgogi	74
불편하다	to be uncomfortable	121
뷔페	buffet	88
비가 오다	to rain.	174
비누	soap	120
비밀 번호	personal identification number	157
비빔밥	Bibimbap	74
비싸다	to be expensive	80
비용	cost	188
비행기	airplane	102
빗	comb	120
빠르다	to be fast	101
빠른우편	express mail	139
빨간색	red color	121
빵	bread	39
뽑다	to pull out	143

ㅅ

Korean	English	Page
사	four	36
사거리	intersection	91
사과	apple	37, 78
사무실	office	29
사이	between	26
사전	dictionary	43
사진	photograph, picture	26, 110
사진기	camera	116
산책을 하다	to take a walk	60
삼	three	36
삼박 사일	3 nights and 4 days	182
색깔	color	119
샐러드	salad	80
생기다	to come up	136
생일	birthday	84
서류 봉투	portfolio	140
서류	documents	140, 195
서비스	service	196
서점	bookstore	42
서쪽	the west	92

선글라스 sunglasses	126	스트레스가 풀리다 to get rid of stress	114
선물 gift	84	스파게티 spaghetti	74
선물하다 to give a present	122	슬리퍼 slippers	126
선생님 teacher	18	시 o'clock	56
선택하다 to choose	143	시간 time	64
설악산 *Seoraksan* (Mt.)	125	시계 watch, clock	25
성함 name (an honorific form of "name")	22, 134	시끄럽다 to be noisy	194
셋 three	36	시다 to be sour	74
셔츠 shirt	120	시설 facilities	196
소나기가 오다 to shower	174	시장 market	27
소독약 disinfectant	170	시청 the city hall	66
소파 sofa	28	시키다 to order	73
소포 parcel	140	식당 restaurant	27
소화제 digestive	170	식사 meal	86
손님 customer	122	식중독 food poisoning	169
송금하다 to wire money online	145, 160	식탁 (dinner) table	29
쇼핑 shopping	59	식혜 *Sikhye*	78
수수료 service charge	155	신나다 to be exciting	109
수업 class	86	신문 newspaper	36
수영 swimming	58, 111	신발가게 footware shop	42
수영을 하다 to swim	59	신분증 ID card	156
수영장 swimming pool	59, 112	신용카드 creditcard	156
수요일 Wednesday	56	신청서 application form	157
수정과 *Sujeonggwa*	78	십 ten	36
수표 check	160	싱가포르 Singapore	178
수프 soup	80	싱싱하다 to be fresh	189
숙박 lodging	188	싸다 to be cheap	106
숙소 place to stay	182	싸다 to wrap	140
쉰 fifty	36	쌀쌀하다 to be chilly	174
슈퍼마켓 supermarket	31	쓰다 to wear (a hat or glasses)	148
스키 ski	110	쓰다 to be bitter	74
스탠드 desk lamp	30		
스테이크 steak	74		

ㅇ

아내 wife	49
아니요 no	45
아래 under	26
아름답다 to be beautiful	188
아버지 father	47, 153
아이스크림 ice cream	36
아홉 nine	36
안 inside	26
안개가 끼다 to be foggy	174
안경 glasses	148
안녕하세요? How are you?	17
앞 in front of	26
애완동물 pet	115
액수 sum	158
야구 baseball	110
약 medicine	171
약속 appointment	64
약속 시간 appointment time	64
약속 장소 appointment place	64
약속하다 to make an appointment	64
약혼식 engagement ceremony	88
얇다 to be thin	120
양말 socks	40
양복 suit	148
양식 Western food	78
양식집 Western restaurant	80
어둡다 to be dark	194
어디 where	25
어떻게 how	101
어떻다 how about	69
어렵다 to be difficult	55
어머니 mother	47, 153
어서 오세요 Welcome	35
어서 right away, with haste	163
언니 elder sister	47
얼마 how much	35
얼마나 how much	96
에어로빅 aerobics	115
에어컨 air conditioner	192
여관 inn	192
여기 here	101
여덟 eight	36
여동생 younger sister	47
여름 summer	174
여섯 six	36
여행 travel	119, 182
여행사 직원 travel agent	18
여행지 destination	182
연기하다 to postpone	64
연필 pencil	30
열 ten	36
열쇠 key	195
열이 나다 to have a fever	164
영국 사람 British	20
영화 movie	110
영화관 movie theater	59
영화를 보다 to watch a movie	59, 63, 110
옆 next to	26
예금하다 to deposit	145
예매하다 to buy in advance	182
예상 경비 estimated budget	182
예약하다 to make a reservation	130, 182
오 five	36
오늘 today	70
오른쪽 right side	92
오빠 elder brother	47
오십 fifty	36

오전 in the morning	64	육교 overpass	92
오후 afternoon	64	은행 bank	27, 155
온돌방 *Ondolbang*	192	은행원 banker	50
온수 hot water	192	음악 music	115
올라가다 to go up	91	음악회 concert	152
옷 clothes	139	의사 doctor	18
옷 가게 clothing store	40	의자 chair	26
옷장 closet	25	이 two	36
왕복 round trip	187	이 this	46
왜 why	71	이가 아프다 to have a toothache	164
왼쪽 the left side	92	이렇게 so, like this	45
요금 (postal) rate	145	이름 name	21
요리사 cook, chef	19	이모 aunt	125
요즘 these days, lately	55	이불 quilt	192
욕실 bathroom	192	이용하다 to use	183
용건 (matter of) business	130	인라인 스케이트 in-line skating	114
우동 *Udong*	75	인삼 ginseng	144
우리 we, our, us	45	일 job, work	19
우산 umbrella	120	일 one	36
우유 milk	39	일곱 seven	36
우체국 post office	141	일본 Japan	18
우체통 postbox	140	일본 사람 Japanese	20
우편 종류 postal type	145	일식 Japanese food	75
우편 mail	143	일요일 Sunday	56
우편물 postal matter	140	일정 schedule	182
우표 stamp	140	읽다 to read	59
운동 sports	109	입금하다 to deposit	160
운동화 sports shoes	120, 150	입다 to wear (clothes)	148
원 won	159	있다 to be there, to exist	25
월요일 Monday	56		
위 above, on	26		
유명하다 to be famous	188	**ㅈ**	
유학 studying abroad	143	자장면 *Jajangmyeon*	75
육 six	36	자전거 bicycle	102

자주 often	78, 117
작다 to be small	121
작성하다 to complete	195
잠그다 to lock	192
잠깐만 for a moment	181
잡지 magazine	40
장 sheet of	37
재미있다 to be interesting	55
저는 I	17
저 that	46
저기 there	147
저녁 evening, dinner	55, 64
전 I	73
전자레인지 microwave	29
전하다 to give (a message)	129
전화번호 phone number	130
전화 telephone	29
전화를 끊다 to ring off	130
전화를 받다 to answer the telephone	130
전화하다 to make a call	130
점원 clerk	35
정도 about	139
정식 table d'hote	80
정오 noon	64
정장 formal suit	88
제 my	83
제일 the most	101
종류 kind	143
좋다 to be good	63
죄송합니다. I'm sorry.	136
주다 to give	35
주말 weekend	56
주부 housewife	18, 49
주사 맞다 to get a (fiu) shot	171

주소 address	157
주식 투자 investment in stocks	160
주유소 gas station	27
준비 preparation	88, 141
중국 China	18
중식 Chinese food	75
즐겁게 지내다 to have a good time	61
증상 symptoms	170
지갑 wallet	122
지불하다 to pay	143
지역 번호 area code	135
지하도 underpass	92
지하철 subway	101
직업 occupation	22
직원 staff	141
직장 workplace	45
집들이 housewarming party	86
짜다 to be salty	74
쪽 side	147
쭉 straight	91
쯤 about, around	63

ㅊ

창문 window	25
찾다 to look for	122
(돈을) 찾다 to withdraw money	158
책 book	26, 55
책상 desk	25
책을 읽다 to read a book	58
책장 bookshelf, bookchest	26
천 thousand	36
첫 번째 first	97
청바지 blue jeans	149

초대장 invitation card	84
초밥 sushi	75
축구 soccer	110
축하 노래 celebratory song	84
출구 exit	107
출금표 withdrawal slip	158
출금하다 to draw out	160
출발하다 to start	182
춥다 to be cold	174
취미 hobby	116
(약속을) 취소하다 to cancel	64
치마 skirt	120
치약 toothpaste	36
치통 toothache	169
친구 friend	55
친구를 만나다 to meet friends	61
칠 seven	36
침대 bed	25
침실 bedroom	192
칫솔 toothbrush	36

클래식 음악 classical music	116

ㅌ

타다 to get on, to take	101
타다 to be tanned	124
탁자 table	30
탕수육 *Tangsuyuk*	75
태권도 *Taegwondo*	55
택시 taxi	102
테니스 치다 to play tennis	70
테니스 tennis	111
텔레비전 television	26
토론토 Toronto	178
토요일 Saturday	56
통장 bankbook	156
통화 중 The line is busy.	130
퇴근하다 to get off and go home from work	163
특급 우편 special delivery mail	143
특히 specially	188

ㅋ

카드 card	84
커피 잔 coffee cup	30
커피 coffee	78
컴퓨터 게임 computer game	113
컴퓨터 computer	29
케이크 cake	84
켜다 to turn on	192
켤레 pair of	37
콘도 condo	192
콧물이 나다 to have runny nose	169
크다 to be big	120

ㅍ

파라솔 parasol	126
파란색 blue color	121
파리 Paris	178
파티 party	86
팔 eight	36
펜션 pension	192
편리하다 to be convenient	161
편안하다 to be comfortable	106
편의점 convenience store	40
편지 letter	140
편하다 to be comfortable	119

포도 grapes	78
포장하다 to wrap	140
프랑스 France	18
프랑스 사람 French	20
피아노 piano	28
필요하다 to need	116, 126

ㅎ

하고 and	25
하나 one	36
하얀색 white color	121
학교 school	59
학생 student	18
한 about	96
한국 Korea	18
한국 사람 Korean	20
한라산 *Hallasan* (Mt.)	188
한식 Korean-style food	74
한식집 Korean restaurant	79
할머니 grandmother	47
할아버지 grandfather	47
해변 beach	188
해수욕장 swimming beach	189
해운대 *Hae-undae*	189
햄버거 hamburger	74
현금 인출기 automatic teller, ATM	161
현금 cash	160
호선 line	101
호주 사람 Australian	20
호텔 hotel	192
홍차 black tea	78
화분 flower pot	30

화요일 Tuesday	56
환율 exchange rate	156
환전하다 to exchange	158
회 sashimi	75, 189
회덮밥 *Hoedeopbap*	80
회비 membership fee, participation fee	88
회사 company	50
회사원 office worker	18, 49
회색 gray color	121
회의 meeting	70, 136
횡단보도 crosswalk	92
후텁지근하다 to be humid	174
휴가 holidays	188
흐리다 to be cloudy	173
히터 heater	192